WINGÅRDHS

FALK JAEGER

JOVIS

PORTFOLIO

WINGÅRDHS

FALK JAEGER

JOVIS

Alle vorgestellten Projekte sind mit Koordinaten versehen, die es erlauben, die Standorte der Gebäude z.B. über GoogleEarth exakt zu lokalisieren. For all projects presented coordinates are provided allowing the exact localisation of the buildings via GoogleEarth or other applications.
© 2010 by jovis Verlag GmbH I Das Copyright für die Texte liegt beim Autor. Das Copyright für die Abbildungen liegt bei den Fotografen/Inhabern der Bildrechte. Texts by kind permission of the author. Pictures by kind permission of the photographers/holders of the picture rights. Die Gesamtreihe Portfolio wird herausgegeben von Falk Jaeger The series Portfolio is edited by Falk Jaeger I Umschlagfoto Cover: vorn front Kuggen, Malmö, hinten back VillAnn, Särö, James Silverman I Alle Renderings, Zeichnungen, Abbildungen und Pläne sind von Wingårdh Arkitektkontor AB All renderings, sketches, illustrations and drawings by Wingårdh Arkitektkontor AB I Fotos Photographs Björn Breitholz 85, 120 I Ulf Celander 14 (l.), 18 (r.), 21 (M. l.), 52, 73, 75, 81, 82, 83, 84 (o.) I Bengt Ericksson 11 (M. r.), 84 (o.), 109–111 I Pål Ericksson 60 (l.) I Hans Gedda 135 I Denis Gillbert/View 94, 96, 97 I Sören Håkanlind 15 (l.) I Stefan Hallberg 34 I Patrik Gunnar Helin 68, 128 I Falk Jaeger 138–143 I Åke E:son Lindman 15 (M.), 19 (r.), 21 (M. r., r.), 27–31, 33, 35 (r.), 38–45, 47, 50, 51 (r.), 53, 61, 62–65, 69, 70, 72, 77–79, 89–93, 107, 114, 115, 117–119, 122-127, 130 (r.), 131–133 I Björn Nilsson 60 (M.) I Mikael Olsson 48, 49 I Michael Perlmutter 130 (l.) I Kimmo Räisänen 56 (o.) I Christian Saltas 66 I James Silverman 98, 100, 101, 103–105, 113 I Nils Olof Sjödén 18 (M. l.) I Jonas Sjögren 10 (r.) I Gert Wingårdh 10 (l., M. l., M. r.), 11 (l., M. l.), 14 (M.), 54, 56 (u.), 57 (o.), 58, 60 (r.) I Wingårdh Arkitektkontor AB and Berg Arkitektenkontor 15 (r.) I Thomas Yeh 35 (l.), 36, 37 I Projekte in Kooperation mit anderen Architekten Projects in cooperation with other architects 15 (M.) Berger + Parkkinen, 15 (r.) Berg Arkitektkontor, 18 (l.) Thomas Sandell, 18 (r.) Mats Matsson and Evata, 19 (l.) Tengboms, 94–97 Thomas Sandell I Alle Rechte vorbehalten. All rights reserved. I Übersetzung Translation: Lucinda Rennison, Berlin I Gestaltung und Satz Design and setting: Susanne Rösler, Berlin I Lithografie Lithography: Bild1Druck, Berlin I Druck und Bindung Printing and binding: GCC Grafisches Centrum Cuno, Calbe I Bibliografische Information der Deutschen Nationalbibliothek Bibliographic information published by Die Deutsche Nationalbibliothek Die Deutsche Nationalbibliothek verzeichnet diese Publikation in der Deutschen Nationalbibliografie; detaillierte bibliografische Daten sind im Internet über http://dnb.d-nb.de abrufbar. Die Deutsche Nationalbibliothek lists this publication in the Deutsche Nationalbibliografie; detailed bibliographic data are available in the Internet at http://dnb.d-nb.de
jovis Verlag GmbH I Kurfürstenstraße 15/16 I 10785 Berlin I www.jovis.de I ISBN 978-3-86859-035-7

INHALT
CONTENTS

Vorwort Foreword   6
Mit allen Sinnen zu erleben   8
To Experience with all the Senses   8

Projekte Projects   25
Müritzeum, Waren (DE)   26
Öijared Executive Country Club, Lerum (SE)   32
Villa bei Amundön, Skintebo (SE)   38
Villa near Amundön, Skintebo (SE)   38
Kajplats 01, Malmö (SE)   42
Auditorium und Studentenwerk der
Technischen Universität Chalmers, Göteborg (SE)   46
Auditorium and Student Union Building of
Chalmers Technical University, Göteborg (SE)   46
Piano Pavillon, Lahti (FI) Piano Pavilion, Lahti (FI)   54
Zitadellenbad, Landskrona (SE)   58
Swimming Pool "Zitadellenbad", Landskrona (SE)   58
Kontrollturm Arlanda International Airport, Sigtuna (SE)   62
Control Tower at Arlanda International Airport, Sigtuna (SE)   62
K:fem Warenhaus, Vällingby (SE)   66
K:fem Department Store, Vällingby (SE)   66
Universeum, Göteborg (SE)   70
Sign Hotel, Stockholm (SE)   76
Knotenpunkt Mölndalbrücke, Mölndal (SE)   80
Junction Mölndal Bridge, Mölndal (SE)   80
AstraZeneca, Mölndal (SE)   82
Schwedische Botschaft, Berlin (DE)   88
Swedish Embassy, Berlin (DE)   88
Ericsson European Headquarters, London (GB)   94
Villa Astrid, Hovås (SE)   98
VillAnn, Särö (SE)   102
Filippa K Ease Store, Stockholm (SE)   106
Villa Nilsson, Varberg (SE)   108
Mühle, Västra Karup (SE) Mill, Västra Karup (SE)   112
Hof Sand, Tofta Kungälv (SE)   116
Sand Farm House, Tofta Kungälv (SE)   116
Ale Kulturzentrum und Gymnasium, Nödinge (SE)   120
Ale Cultural Centre and Grammar School, Nödinge (SE)   120
Villa Roser, Skara (SE)   124
Schwedisches Haus, Washington DC (USA)   128
House of Sweden, Washington DC (USA)   128

Mitarbeiter Collaborators   134
Der Architekt The Architect   135
Vierzehn Fragen Fourteen Questions   137

VORWORT
FOREWORD

Schwedische Architektur ist präzise, korrekt, qualitätvoll – und langweilig. Diese Erkenntnis hatte sich nach den sechziger Jahren, als die Studenten europäischer Hochschulen noch zu Architekturexkursionen nach Schweden aufgebrochen waren, in den siebziger und achtziger Jahren nach und nach verdichtet. Gert Wingårdh ist einer der wenigen Architekten, die dieses Vorurteil nun gründlich ausräumen. Bei ihm gibt es immer etwas zu sehen und zu staunen. Er ist seit vielen Jahren wieder einmal ein schwedischer Baukünstler, der außerhalb seines Landes und außerhalb Skandinaviens wahrgenommen wird.

Dabei ist es schwierig, sich ein Bild von seiner Architektur zu machen. Wingårdh steht nicht für eine bestimmte Art von Architektur. Auch der Kenner hat kaum eine Chance, ein Gebäude von ihm zu identifizieren, denn nichts scheint er mehr zu verabscheuen, als einmal „verbrauchte" Lösungsmöglichkeiten aus seinem Fundus neuerlich zu verwenden. Vielleicht ist er der ideale Architekt, der in der Lage ist, jede Aufgabe bei null anzufangen, eigene Vorurteile, Vorprägungen, Vorlieben hintanzustellen und die einzige, einzigartige, eigentümliche Lösung zu entwickeln. „Architektur ist immer die Errichtung konkreter Bauwerke, nicht eines vagen Theoriegebäudes", schrieb Henry Russell Hitchcock 1932 in *The International Style*. Wingårdh geht es in jedem Einzelfall um dieses konkrete Bauwerk. Konsequenterweise verweigert er deshalb die Definition einer eigenen theoretischen Position. Er will sich nicht festlegen (lassen).

Man ist versucht, bei der Auseinandersetzung mit Wingårdhs Architektur den Begriff „Form" zu vermeiden, denn selten geht es bei Wingårdh um Formfindung oder Formgestaltung (wenngleich er, seinem pluralistischen Ansatz gemäß, Formalismen nicht völlig verabscheut). Er entwirft keine Monumente, im Gegenteil, er ver-

Swedish architecture is precise, correct, high-quality—and tedious. After the sixties, when students from European universities were still embarking on architectural excursions to Sweden, this judgement gradually developed and intensified during the seventies and eighties. Gert Wingårdh is one of the few architects who are thoroughly doing away with such preconceived notions. There is always something in his work to catch the eye and to be astonished by. For many years now, this has been one architect from Sweden whose work is attracting attention outside his own country, and even outside Scandinavia.

Yet it is difficult to gain an impression of his work: Wingårdh does not stand for any particular kind of architecture. Even the experts have little chance of being able to identify one of his buildings, for there appears to be nothing he despises more than re-using a solution from his collection once it has been "expended". Perhaps he is the ideal architect, in a position to start from scratch for every assignment, putting his own preconceptions, imprinting, and preferences behind him and developing the one and only, unique, and idiosyncratic solution. "Architecture is always a set of actual monuments, not a vague corpus of theory", as Henry Russell Hitchcock wrote in *The International Style* in 1932. In every individual case, Gert Wingårdh is concerned with that actual structure. He consistently refuses, therefore, to give a definition of his own theoretical position; he does not wish to pin himself down (or let himself be pinned down).

It is tempting when examining Wingårdh's architecture to avoid the concept of "form", for Wingårdh's work is rarely a matter of finding or designing form (although in accordance with his pluralist starting point, he does not entirely despise formalisms). He does not design monuments; on the contrary, sometimes he even deliberately con-

steckt die Gebäude manchmal bewusst, da ihm die vorgefundene Situation wichtiger ist als die Manifestation seiner Arbeit. Er tritt nicht an, a priori „großartige Bauwerke" zu schaffen – und schafft sie doch, in anderem Sinn.

Nicht die Form oder die Dekoration, sondern wie die Menschen in seinen Bauten leben, das ist der Maßstab seines Entwerfens und er scheint sich damit an Philibert de l'Orme zu halten, der schon 1567 fand: „Die Bequemlichkeit, der Gebrauchswert und der Nutzen für die Bewohner sind für ein Haus wichtiger als die schönsten Proportionen und Verzierungen."

Die Menschen sollen sich nicht den Häusern anpassen müssen, sondern die Häuser sollen sich den Bewohnern zuwenden. John Ruskin hatte formuliert, was die Menschen von ihren Häusern erwarten. Die Häuser sollen Schutz geben und mit ihnen reden – sollen Stimmungen vermitteln, Anregungen und Erinnerungen. Vor allem Wingårdhs Wohnhäuser und Villen vermögen diese Bedürfnisse auf ideale Weise im Kleinen zu erfüllen. Sie erzählen ganze Geschichten und inszenieren kleine Dramen. Wingårdhs Sozialbauten wirken auf gleiche Weise im Großen. Sie sind nicht nur Ableistung von Planerfüllung und Bereitstellung normierten Raums für vorgegebene Funktionen. Sie bieten Schutz und Identifikation – sie sind Orte der Selbsterfahrung und bieten Raum für soziale Aktivitäten.

Von Wingårdh lernen, heißt also nicht, seine Prinzipien zu erfassen und seine Lehrsätze auswendig zu lernen. Wingårdh ist ein pragmatischer Lehrer, an der Universität wie in der Praxis durch sein gebautes Werk. Gert Wingårdhs Œuvre kennenzulernen, ist eine Abenteuerreise in das vielfältige Land der Architektur, die immer neue Überraschungen mit sich bringt. Dieses JOVIS Portfolio versucht sich als Führer für diese Abenteuerreise. Die Reise selbst kann es nicht ersetzen.

ceals his buildings, as the situation that he finds is more important to him than a manifestation of his work. He does not start out *a priori* to create "outstanding buildings"—and yet in a different sense, that is just what he ends up doing.

The measure of Wingårdh's planning is not the form or embellishment of his buildings, but how people live in them, and he seems to agree in this respect with Philibert de l'Orme, who had already determined in 1567 that: "The comfort, convenience and advantage of the inhabitants are more important in a house than beautiful proportions and rich decorations."

People should not have to adapt to their houses; on the contrary, houses should be oriented towards their inhabitants. John Ruskin set out those things that people expect from their homes: houses should offer protection and communicate with their inhabitants—they should convey moods, stimuli and memories. On a small scale, Gert Wingårdh's private houses and villas in particular manage to fulfil these needs ideally. They tell complete stories and stage minor dramas. Wingårdh's public buildings have the same effect on a bigger scale. They not only fulfil plans and provide standardised spaces for given functions, they also offer protection and identification—they are places to experience the self and also provide space for social activities.

Learning from Wingårdh, therefore, does not mean understanding his principles and committing his theorems to memory. Wingårdh is a pragmatic teacher, both at the university and in practice, via his constructed work. Getting to know Gert Wingårdh's oeuvre represents a voyage of discovery to the varied land of architecture, where fresh surprises always lie in wait. This JOVIS Portfolio endeavours to be a guide on that voyage of discovery, but it cannot replace the journey itself.

MIT ALLEN SINNEN ZU ERLEBEN
TO EXPERIENCE WITH ALL THE SENSES

Gert Wingårdh ist zweifellos ein den Freuden des Lebens zugewandter Mensch. Er kennt die Plätze seiner Heimatstadt, an denen man die besten Langostinos und den delikatesten Käse kauft, und im Restaurant des Kunstmuseums lässt es sich der Koch nicht nehmen, ihn persönlich zu begrüßen. Er schätzt seinen Sportwagen deutscher Provenienz und er kann ohne Flachbildschirm allerorts nicht leben. Man ahnt, dass die Sinnlichkeit, die den meisten seiner Bauten zu eigen ist, etwas mit seiner Persönlichkeit zu tun haben muss.

Diese für einen Schweden nicht gerade genuine Art ist umso erstaunlicher, als Gert Wingårdh zumindest bis vor wenigen Jahren eine frappierende Sesshaftigkeit an den Tag gelegt hat. Geboren in Skövde, 140 Kilometer landeinwärts, studierte er in Göteborg, arbeitete bei Olivegrens in Göteborg, gründete sein Büro in Göteborg und wurde Professor und Vorsitzender des Lenkungsausschusses des Fachbereichs Architektur an seiner Heimatuniversität. Da war es dann geradezu ein beherzter Schritt, ein Zweigbüro in Stockholm zu gründen.

Dennoch gilt er nicht als typisch schwedischer Architekt. Von Anbeginn bestens international informiert und orientiert, hat er seine Einflüsse und Anregungen immer überall dort hergeholt, wo sie ihm brauchbar schienen. Er ist „einer der lebendigsten und kreativsten schwedischen Architekten, der aus der engstirnigen bürokratischen schwedischen Norm ausbricht und überraschend andere, entzückende und bestens ausgeführte Bauten liefert", urteilte Peter Blundell Jones in einem Text für das englische Magazin *Architectural Review*.

Wie seine selbstständige Arbeit angefangen hat? Mit kleinen Aufträgen, Innenarchitektur für Läden, Restaurants und mit der Villa Hansson in Göteborg Fis-

kebäck, errichtet 1977 im Jahr der Bürogründung. Das von Charles Moores Sea Ranch in Kalifornien inspirierte Haus besteht aus zwei holzverkleideten, im spitzen Winkel zueinander gestellten Baukörpern. Mit niedrigem Budget ist es aus Sperrholz gebaut, zeigt aber schon manches Merkmal späterer Villenentwürfe Wingårdhs, den räumlichen Überraschungseffekt nach dem Eintreten, die Einbettung in die Felsen, den Kontrast zwischen hellen, offenen und wärmeren, geborgenen Räumen.

Die Gestaltung von Leoni's Salad Bar war die erste innenarchitektonische Aufgabe. Eine verspiegelte, gerade Wand einerseits und eine ondulierende Wand aus Glasbausteinen andererseits begrenzen physisch und entgrenzen optisch das Volumen des Restaurants. „Wenn nicht einem Borromini angemessen, so doch wenigstens einem Portoghesi", charakterisierte Wingårdh verschmitzt den pulsierenden Raum und bezog sich damit auf den Barockarchitekten und den damals aktuellen postmodernen Italiener gleichermaßen.

Leoni's teilte das Schicksal vieler kurzlebiger, kommerzieller Interieurs ebenso wie das 1979 entstandene Marmite Restaurant in Åre, das erst 2009 neu dekoriert wurde. Es besaß ebenfalls verspiegelte Wände und die flach gewölbten Decken verbreiteten ein sanftes, indirektes Licht.

Der Auftrag zum Umbau und zur Modernisierung des Hotels Kramer in Malmö war dann eine umfängliche Arbeit, die andere Aufträge zur Folge hatte. Wingårdh wurde damals (und noch 1998 in der großen Schweden-Ausstellung im Deutschen Architekturmuseum Frankfurt am Main, inzwischen doch wohl zu Unrecht) ganz und gar den postmodernen Architekten zugerechnet. Das hatte vor allem mit der Villa Nordh zu tun, die er 1978–81 in Göteborg

There is certainly no doubt that Gert Wingårdh is a man ready to enjoy the pleasures of life. In his home town, he knows where to buy the best langoustines and the most delicious cheese, and the cook of the Art Museum's restaurant is intent on welcoming him personally. He appreciates his German sports car and he cannot live without flat screens, either at home or work. It seems likely that the sensuality which characterises most of his buildings is rooted in his personality.

This is not exactly the original Swedish way, and is all the more astonishing as Gert Wingårdh—at least until a few years ago—had always shown a remarkably settled approach to life. Born in Skövde, 140 kilometres inland, he studied in Göteborg, worked at Olivegrens in Göteborg, founded his office in Göteborg, and became a professor and Chairman of the Steering Board of the Architectural Section at the university in his home town. So it was a remarkably bold step even to found a branch of his office in Stockholm.

Nevertheless, he is not regarded as a typical Swedish architect. Well-informed and internationally oriented from the very beginning, he has always looked for influences and stimuli wherever they appear usable to him. He is "one of the most lively and creative architects in Sweden, breaking through the hidebound and bureaucratised Swedish norm with a series of surprisingly diverse, exciting and well executed buildings," according to Peter Blundell Jones in a text for the English magazine *Architectural Review*.

How did his independent work begin? It began gradually with small commissions, interior design for shops or restaurants, and with Villa Hansson in Göteborg Fiskebäck, built in 1977—the year that he founded his office. This house inspired by Charles Moore's Sea Ranch in California consists of two wood-clad volumes set at sharp angles to one another. Built from plywood on a low budget, nonetheless it already demonstrates some features of later villa designs by Wingårdh: the surprising effect of space upon entering, its embedding in the rocks and the contrast between bright, open and other warmer, cosy rooms.

Leoni's Salad Bar was his first interior design assignment. The volume of the restaurant is physically delineated and optically delimited by a straight wall of mirrors on one side and an undulating wall of glass bricks on the other. "If not worthy of a Borromini then at any rate of a Porthogesi," Wingårdh commented tongue in cheek, characterising this pulsating space and so referring to both the baroque master and the post-modern Italian architect, who was very much "in" at the time.

Leoni's shared the fate of many short-lived commercial interiors, like the Marmite Restaurant in Åre, designed in 1979—although this was not redecorated until 2009. It also had mirrored walls and a soft, indirect light emanating from gently bulging ceilings. The subsequent contract to convert and modernise Hotel Kramer in Malmö was an extensive project leading on to others. At that time Wingårdh was categorised completely and utterly as a post-modern architect (and this was still the case in the big Sweden exhibition in the German Museum of Architecture in Frankfurt am Main in 1998, although by then it was probably no longer true). First and foremost, this attribution was a result of Villa Nordh, which he built in Göteborg in 1978–81. This had been celebrated as the first post-modern house in Sweden. Wingårdh had just returned from the USA, where he

baute und die man als das erste postmoderne Haus Schwedens gefeiert hatte. Wingårdh war gerade aus den USA zurückgekommen, wo er auch Mother´s House von Venturi bestaunt hatte, und verarbeitete die Eindrücke postwendend. Eine besondere Legitimation für die in Bogen die Fassade überziehenden hölzernen Rankgitter benötigte er nicht, er nahm sich einfach die Freiheit – und wurde deshalb auch heftig kritisiert.

Vielleicht hat er die Vorwürfe ernst genommen oder er nahm den Trend der folgenden Zeit frühzeitig wahr, jedenfalls vergaß er das kurzweilige postmoderne Formenrepertoire (mit kleinen Rückfällen im innenarchitektonischen Bereich) bald wieder, nicht

gangsgeschoss als Anregung und zum Anlass und machte sie zur Grundform des Entwurfs. Als hätte ihn die Lust getrieben, einmal das Thema in allen Variationen durchzuspielen, ließ er alles zirkulieren: den Empfang und die Bar, die Lobby, die Theken und die Deckenspiegel, die Toilettenvorräume und die Garderoben, alles schwingend und ineinander übergehend. Selbst die Treppe ins Erdgeschoss hinab gestaltete er kreisförmig, eine konkav-konvexe Treppe mit rundem Mittelpodest, wie man sie zuletzt im französischen Barock gesehen hat. Als Blickfang beim Eintritt stellte er die Scandic Crown, eine goldene Krone, auf einer Marmorsäule zur Schau. In den Zimmern war vornehm beruhigtes Design nicht

RESTAURANT LEONI'S, GÖTEBORG (SE) RESTAURANT LEONI'S, GÖTEBORG (SE) LAURA ASHLEY SHOP, STOCKHOLM (SE) LAURA ASHLEY SHOP, STOCKHOLM (SE) VILLA HANSSON, GÖTEBORG (SE) VILLA HANSSON, GÖTEBORG (SE) SCANDIC CROWN HOTEL, STOCKHOLM (SE) SCANDIC CROWN HOTEL, STOCKHOLM (SE)

jedoch die Errungenschaften der Postmoderne, denn Geschichten erzählen wollte er mit seiner Architektur nach wie vor. Bereits 1982 sagte er dann in einem Interview: „Die Prinzipien des Funktionalismus sind ohne Einschränkung vereinbar mit der Forderung, dass jedes Gebäude Lust machen muss, es anzuschauen."

Höhepunkt der von der Innenarchitektur bestimmten Periode seines Schaffens in den achtziger Jahren war 1986 sein Auftrag, das von Mats Edblom errichtete Scandic Crown Hotel in Stockholm (heute Hilton Stockholm Slussen) einzurichten. Wingårdh nahm die Kreisform der Vorfahrt im oberen Ein-

gefragt. Die Wände bekleidete er mit lebhaft kontrastierenden Holzpaneelen. Geflammte Birke, tiefrotes Kirschholz und italienische Walnuss treten in alternierenden Streifen vor Augen. Dieses Hotel sollte auch den Vielfliegern unter den Gästen im Gedächtnis bleiben. Unter dem neuen Betreiber ist das Interieur dann teilweise verändert, vor allem beruhigt und dem „internationalen Geschmack" angeglichen worden.

Für Laura Ashley in Stockholm war 1984 ein kleines Ladengeschäft für Brautmoden entstanden, in dem für den Charakter und die Stimmung ebenfalls das Holzfurnier der Möbel und das Parkett die entschei-

had admired Mother´s House by Venturi and implemented the impressions gained in his work straight away. He did not require any specific legitimacy for the climbing wooden grille that covered the façade in an arc, he simply acted freely—and was much criticised for it.

Perhaps he took this reproof seriously, or he had perceived the trend of the subsequent period very early on; but certainly he soon forgot the diverting post-modern repertoire of forms (with minor relapses in the area of interior design), although not the achievements of Post-Modernism—since he continued his desire to tell stories with architecture. As early as 1982, he said in an interview: "The princi-

ceiling mirrors, the vestibules to the toilets and the cloakrooms, everything curved and permeating into each other. He even designed the staircase down to the ground floor as a circle: a concave-convex stairway with a round central rostrum like the ones last seen in the French Baroque. As an eye-catcher when entering, he displayed the Scandic Crown—a golden crown—on a marble pillar. There was no demand for noble, tranquil design in the rooms, so he clad the walls in lively, contrasting wooden panels. Flamed birch, deep red cherry wood and Italian walnut appear in alternating stripes. The aim was to engrave this hotel into the memory of even frequent flyers among the guests. Under the new operators,

VILLA HANSSON, GÖTEBORG (SE) VILLA HANSSON, GÖTEBORG (SE) VILLA NORDH, GÖTEBORG (SE) VILLA NORDH, GÖTEBORG (SE) VILLA NILSSON, VARBERG (SE) VILLA NILSSON, VARBERG (SE) BESUCHERZENTRUM NATURUM, TÅKERN (SE), RENDERING VISITOR CENTRE NATURUM, TÅKERN (SE), RENDERING

ples of functionalism are perfectly compatible with insisting that buildings must be fun to look at."

The high point of this period of his oeuvre defined by interior design during the eighties was his commission, in 1986, to furnish the Scandic Crown Hotel in Stockholm (today the Hilton Stockholm Slussen), built by Mats Edblom. Wingårdh took the circular form of the covered, first-floor entrance area as an impetus and starting point, making it the basic form of his design. As if he had suddenly been taken by a desire to play out this theme with all its variations, he turned everything into circles: the reception desk and the bar, the lobby, the counters and the

the interior has been altered in parts; above all, it has been toned down and adapted to "international taste".

He designed a small bridal wear shop for Laura Ashley in Stockholm in 1984, where the wooden varnish of the furnishings and parquet floor also played a key role in its character and atmosphere. This atmosphere was reminiscent of interiors by Adolf Loos in Vienna during the nineteen-twenties. In order to connect the four narrow rooms arranged in a rectangle, Wingårdh simply cut out the crossing point of their walls. The cut-off brick walls were then glazed using a golden-red shimmering paint.

dende Rolle spielten. Die Atmosphäre erinnerte an die Interieurs von Adolf Loos im Wien der zwanziger Jahre. Um die vier engen, im Karree angeordneten Räume miteinander zu verbinden, schnitt Wingårdh einfach den Kreuzungspunkt der Wände heraus. Die angeschnittenen Ziegelwände ließ er mit einer gold-rot schimmernden Farbe lackieren.

Laura Ashley in Stockholm ist ebenso wenig erhalten geblieben wie Wingårdhs Arbeit für Yoko Yap 1982 in Göteborg. Wieder schlüpfte Wingårdh spielend in eine neue Rolle und entwarf für das japanische Schuhgeschäft ein kühl-modernistisches, fast zeitloses Ambiente, das mit wenigen Anklängen unzweifelhaft japanisch anmutete. Da sind die hinterleuchteten Regalwände, die an japanische Papierwände erinnern, die in liegende Formate unterteilten Glas- und Wandflächen, die harten Kontraste heller Felder und schwarzer Rahmen, und da ist die Gliederung des Fußbodens in einzelne Felder, die an traditionelle japanische Räume mit Tatami-Matten erinnert. Die beiden leicht schräg gestellten Tresen aus Sichtbeton entzogen sich der grafisch dominierenden, ansonsten alles bestimmenden geometrisch-rechteckigen Gliederung. Seit dem Umzug des Ladens einige Häuser weiter im Jahr 2007 präsentiert sich Yoko Yap in einem neutral weißen Ladenlokal – mit Kronleuchter an der Decke.

Naturum Tåkern ist ein Vogelschutzgebiet am Südufer des Tåkernsees in Östergötland. Das Besucherzentrum zeigt nach außen keine Fassaden, sondern nur Strohdachflächen, um es in die Natur einzufügen. Im Grundriss zitiert es die Form des Dreiseithofes. Wie auf Zehenspitzen steht es aufgeständert im Grund des Feuchtgebietes. Auch der Beobachtungsturm nahebei ist mit einer Strohfassade verkleidet. Die Besucher erreichen ihn über eine durch die Kronen der Bäume mäandrierende Holzbrücke.

Der Quantensprung für das Büro Wingårdh kam 1989 mit dem Auftrag für den Laborcampus von Astra Hässle in Mölndal, der jungen Industriestadt, zehn Minuten südlich von Göteborg. Damit wuchs er innerhalb weniger Jahre von der Innenarchitektur in die Welt der Großaufträge hinein. Wingårdh

gewann trotz fehlender Erfahrung im Laborbau den eingeladenen Wettbewerb und hatte die nächsten acht Jahre seine Arbeitskraft zu 80 Prozent Astra zu widmen. Trotzdem entstanden in dieser Zeit nicht weniger als 56 weitere Projekte. Urlaub hat er damals nicht gemacht, als er sich noch jung, aber schon erfahren und leistungsfähig fühlte. AstraZeneca, wie der Pharmakonzern später firmierte, brachte ihm 1993 den zweiten Kasper Salin Preis ein, was er als Beweis dafür ansah, dass der erste Erfolg mit dem Golfklub Öijared keine Eintagsfliege war.

War Wingårdh im Wirtschaftsraum an der Westküste von Anbeginn präsent, so musste er sich das Verwaltungs- und Regierungszentrum Stockholm erst erschließen. Die Regierungsaufträge in der zweiten Hälfte der neunziger Jahre für die Botschaft in Berlin, das Stadion für die Bewerbung Stockholms für die Olympischen Spiele 2004 und den Kontrollturm Arlanda öffneten ihm dort die Türen und machten ihn hoffähig. Im Jahr 2000 wurde er direkt für die Regierung tätig, als er im Stockholmer Tigern Quartier ein Verwaltungszentrum für das Landwirtschafts- und das Sozialministerium, das aus mehreren Gebäuden des 19. und 20. Jahrhunderts besteht, sanierte und mit einem überglasten Lichthof ausstattete.

Inzwischen kennt man ihn nicht nur in Schweden als einen der einflussreichsten und erfolgreichsten skandinavischen Architekten. Natürlich wurde die großartige Schwedische Botschaft in Washington in amerikanischen Fachkreisen aufmerksam registriert. Aber auch seine Arbeiten für alle Big Player, die über Schweden hinaus einen Namen haben wie Volvo, Ericsson oder Astra und schließlich die wachsende Anzahl seiner Bauten und Projekte im Ausland machten ihn international präsent. Mittlerweile ist ihm der Weg zum Flughafen fast so geläufig wie der vom Haus zum Büro in der Kungsgatan. Dort, im Bürobau aus den dreißiger Jahren, hat sich das Büro Schritt für Schritt in fast alle Geschosse ausgebreitet und greift schon ins Nachbarhaus über. Es gibt kaum größere Büroräume, dafür viele kleine Zimmer mit Ausblicken auf Nachbargassen und Dächer, insgesamt ein labyrinthisches System,

Laura Ashley in Stockholm has not survived any more than Wingårdh's work for Yoko Yap in Göteborg in 1982. Again, Wingårdh slipped playfully into a new role and designed a cool, modernistic, almost timeless ambience for the Japanese shoe store, which employs only a few echoes to appear unmistakably Japanese: there are backlit walls of shelves that suggest Japanese paper walls, glass and wall areas divided into long, flat sections, harsh contrasts between light areas and black frames, and there is the division of the floor into single fields, which is reminiscent of traditional Japanese rooms with tatami mats. The two slightly oblique counters made of exposed concrete evaded the graphically dominant, otherwise all-determining geometric-rectangular layout. Since the store's move a few buildings further along in 2007, Yoko Yap has been a neutral white shop—with a chandelier hanging from the ceiling.

Naturum Tåkern is a bird sanctuary on the southern shore of Lake Tåkern in East Gothland. The visitor centre has no visible façades, only areas of thatched roof which allow it to merge with its natural surroundings. The ground plan echoes the form of a three-sided farmyard. It perches on stilts on the ground of the wetlands as if on tiptoe. The façade of the observation tower nearby is also clad in thatch. Visitors reach it via a wooden bridge meandering through the treetops.

For the Wingårdh Office, the quantum leap came in 1989 with a contract for the laboratory campus of Astra Hässle in Mölndal, the young industrial town ten minutes south of Göteborg. In this way, Wingårdh progressed from interior design to the world of major commissions within a few years. Despite his lack of experience in the construction of laboratories, Wingårdh won the competition among invited submissions and over the next eight years he was compelled to devote 80 per cent of his labour power to Astra. Nevertheless, during this period he completed no less than fifty-six other projects. At that time he took no holidays, still feeling young but already experienced and capable of great achievements. AstraZeneca, as the pharmaceutical concern was later known, brought him the second Kasper Salin Prize in 1993, which he regarded as proof of the fact that his first success with Öijared Golf Club was more than a flash in the pan.

Although Wingårdh had a place and reputation in the west-coast economy from the beginning, he had to make inroads into Stockholm and its administrative and governmental centres later on. The government contracts in the second half of the nineties—for the Berlin embassy, the stadium for Stockholm's application for the 2004 Olympic Games, and the control tower at Arlanda—opened doors to him and gave him a name "at court". In 2000 he worked directly for the government when he renewed an administration centre for the Ministry of Agriculture and Social Affairs in Stockholm's Tigern district and provided it with an atrium with a glazed-over roof. The centre comprised several buildings from the nineteenth and twentieth centuries.

It is not just in Sweden that Wingårdh is known as one of the most influential and successful Scandinavian architects. Naturally, the magnificent Swedish embassy in Washington has been noticed in specialist American circles. But his work for all the "big players" whose names are well-known beyond Sweden like Volvo, Ericsson or Astra, and finally the growing number of buildings and projects abroad have also made him internationally prominent. In the meantime, he has become almost as familiar with the route to the airport as he is with that from his house to the office in Kungsgatan. There, in a commercial building dating from the thirties, his office has expanded step by step onto almost all the floors and is beginning to cross into the neighbouring property. There are very few larger offices, but many small rooms with views out over neighbouring alleyways and roofs; overall, it is a labyrinthine system, in which the surrounding old city is always present as a scale-generating space. Around ninety employees in the Göteborg office work to realise his ideas in the constructed environment, and there are thirty more in Stockholm.

in dem die umgebende Altstadt als räumliche, Maßstab gebende Sphäre immer präsent ist. Rund 90 Mitarbeiter arbeiten im Büro Göteborg daran, seine Ideen in gebaute Umwelt umzusetzen, weitere 30 in Stockholm.

Wingårdh ist kein Mannschaftsspieler, kein *primus inter pares*. Nicht jeden Entwurf kann er von der Idee bis zur Fertigstellung intensiv begleiten, aber er legt Wert darauf, alle Projekte unter Kontrolle zu halten. Und noch immer füllt er das Skizzenbuch mit seinen Zeichnungen und Notizen. Den Schritt zum alles beherrschenden Computer hat er nicht vollzogen. Das sinnliche Erlebnis des Arbeitens mit dem Zeichenstift, das er vor der Computerzeit so intensiv und

ist in allen Sätteln gerecht, beherrscht alle Spiel- und Stilarten und alle Typologien. Beispielsweise ist ein größerer Gegensatz kaum denkbar als der zwischen seinem Hof Sand und der VillAnn, die beide in ähnlicher Situation am Ufer mit Seeblick liegen. Hier der atmosphärisch aufgeladene, alle Lichtstimmungen auskostende, örtliche Tradition, Geborgenheit und Naturverbundenheit zelebrierende nonchalante Landsitz, dort das prototypisch kühlabstrakte, perfektionistische Artefakt im Stil der internationalen Moderne. Ralph Erskine einerseits, Tadao Ando andererseits, so könnte man die Pole mit den Namen bekannter Protagonisten benennen. Beide gegensätzlichen Ausprägungen des Wohn- und Lebens-

PARKHAUS ASTRAZENECA, MÖLNDAL (SE) PARKING GARAGE ASTRAZENECA, MÖLNDAL (SE) YOKO YAP SHOP, GÖTEBORG (SE) YOKO YAP SHOP, GÖTEBORG (SE) VILLA QUOOGE, LONG ISLAND (USA), RENDERING VILLA QUOOGE, LONG ISLAND (USA), RENDERING

akribisch betrieben hat, möchte er nicht missen. Er war sich immer der Macht des Bildes, der Überzeugungskraft von Schaubildern vor allem für Laien, für Bauherren bewusst, damals, als er selbst dramatische, an Piranesi erinnernde Veduten gezeichnet hat und heute, wo die hinreißendsten Visualisierungen digital im Computer erzeugt werden. Die piranesiartigen Perspektiven sind Computervisualisierungen von gleicher Emotionalität und ähnlicher Anmutung gewichen, die den Betrachtern die intensiven imaginären Raumerlebnisse vermitteln sollen.

Vergleicht man die verschiedenen Arbeiten Wingårdhs miteinander, gewinnt man den Eindruck, er

gefühls weiß er mit seiner Architektur perfekt zu bedienen.

Es hat etwas Spielerisches, wie er sich der Seriosität einer sorgsam definierten architektonischen Haltung entzieht und bei jedem Projekt immer wieder neue Anregungen heranzieht, neue Ideen entwickelt, um vor allem eines zu erreichen: dem Ort, dem Nutzen und dem Benutzer gerecht zu werden. Wingårdh erwähnt in diesem Zusammenhang gern die Schweizer Kollegen Herzog & de Meuron, die gleichermaßen unvoreingenommen an jede neue Aufgabe herantreten und deren Werk deshalb von ähnlicher Variabilität gekennzeichnet ist.

Wingårdh is not a team player, not *a primus inter pares*. He is not able to supervise every design intensely from the idea to its completion, but he regards it as important to keep all projects under his constant control. And he still continues to fill a sketchbook with his drawings and notes. He has not yet completed the transition to the all-dominant computer. He does not wish to sacrifice the sensual experience of working with pencil or pen, which he did so extensively and meticulously before the computer age. He has always been aware of the power of the image, the power of conviction that visual demonstrations convey, especially to the layman, to the building clients. In the past, he drew

in similar coastal locations with a view of the sea. The first is a highly atmospheric country estate in local tradition, exploiting every mood of the light, celebrating cosiness and closeness to nature, and the second is the prototypically, coolly abstract perfectionist artefact in the style of international Modernism. Ralph Erskine on the one hand and Tadao Ando on the other—or so the two poles might be labelled with names of well-known protagonists. He is capable of making his architecture accord perfectly with the two opposite lifestyles and approaches to life.

There is something rather playful about the way that he evades the seriousness of a neatly defined

  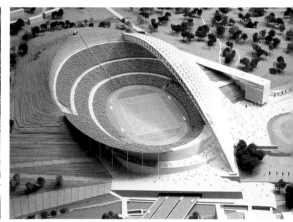

UNIVERSEUM, GÖTEBORG (SE) UNIVERSEUM, GÖTEBORG (SE) SCHWEDISCHE BOTSCHAFT, BERLIN (DE) SWEDISH EMBASSY, BERLIN (DE) VICTORIA OLYMPIASTADION, STOCKHOLM (SE) VICTORIA OLYMPIC STADIUM, STOCKHOLM (SE)

dramatic city views reminiscent of Piranesi whilst today, the most delightful visualisations can be created digitally using the computer: Piranesi-like perspectives have given way to computer visualisations, which, with the same emotionality and a similar appearance, convey imaginary but intense 3-D experiences to the observer.

Comparing Wingårdh's different works to one another, one gets the impression that he can saddle almost any horse—that he has mastered all methods, styles and typologies. A greater contrast is scarcely imaginable, for example, than the one between his country estate Sand and VillAnn, although both are

architectonic standpoint and is always seeking out new stimuli, new ideas for every new project, aiming to achieve one thing first and foremost: to do justice to the setting, the usage, and the user. In this context, Wingårdh likes to cite his Swiss colleagues Herzog & de Meuron, who approach each new task with the same lack of partiality and whose work is therefore characterised by comparable variability.

However, many projects do have something in common, something that plays a part—if not the main part—in his villas. This is Wingårdh's irrepressible desire for a truly theatrical staging of the landscape

Es gibt allerdings bei vielen Projekten eine Gemeinsamkeit, die insbesondere bei den Villen eine Rolle, wenn nicht die Hauptrolle spielt. Dies ist Wingårdhs unbändige Lust an der geradezu theatralischen Inszenierung der vorgefundenen Landschaft durch die Kulisse des Hauses. Die VillAnn öffnet sich auf ganzer Breite der Nachmittags- und Abendsonne wie eine Bühne, um auch den letzten Lichtstrahl einzufangen – und lässt die Passanten auf der Uferstraße an ihrem Leben teilhaben. Ähnlich beim Hof Sand, wo die vierte Wand zum Meer hin durch die rahmenlose Aussicht ersetzt ist. Die Villa Nilsson und die Villa vor Amundön zelebrieren das Panorama auf unterschiedliche Weise als Architektur- und Landschaftserlebnis. In der Villa Astrid erlebt man die räumliche Befreiung, nachdem man in beengter Situation von oben in das Haus gekommen ist und in den sich weitenden Raum hinabsteigt.

Ein ortsbezogenes Thema, das Gert Wingårdh bei der Auseinandersetzung mit der Topografie des Grundstücks gern aufgreift, ist der gewachsene Fels, wie er auf Bauplätzen in Schwedens Küstenregionen oft genug anzutreffen ist. Mit dem von ihm favorisierten heimischen Kalkstein ist Wingårdh schon in jungen Jahren beim Spielen in der Natur und in der Fabrik seines Vaters in Berührung gekommen und davon geprägt worden. Die Landschaft ist für ihn Wohnort, der Mensch archaisch mit der Erde verwachsen. Seine Häuser erheben sich nicht, um sich vom Baugrund zu distanzieren, sie schmiegen sich an, graben sich ein, werden eins mit dem Ort. Oft fügen sich die Häuser in die Felsformationen, oft wachsen die Felsen ins Haus und vermitteln den Bewohnern das beruhigende Gefühl des Verwurzelt-Seins. In der Villa Astrid oder in der Villa Nilsson wachsen die Felsen ins Haus und „erden" es. Beim Universeum in Göteborg konnte er das Thema nochmals in großem Stil abhandeln. Das Gebäude ist auf den Fels gebaut, der Berg mit einem überdimensionalen Gewächshaus überwölbt, in dessen Schutz sich Fauna und Flora unter tropischen Bedingungen entwickeln können. Dort, wo künstlich weiterzubauen ist, abstrahiert er den gewachsenen Felsen mit seinen Gesteinsschichten. Er schichtet seinerseits Stein in Form von Platten und Trittstufen, die er nicht akkurat zu Treppenläufen übereinander setzt, sondern – wie zum Beispiel in der Villa Nilsson – freier arrangiert, eine natürliche Situation künstlerisch überhöhend. Beim Golfklub Öijared hat er im Inneren die Berglandschaft künstlerisch interpretiert. Geometrischer erscheint die Freitreppe vor der Villa bei Amundön. Aber auch das Setzen einer schlichten Trittstufe am Hof Sand geschieht nicht ohne eine solche Überlegung. Hier und da fühlt man sich an Carlo Scarpa erinnert, der zu Wingårdhs Favoriten zählt.

Es gibt Architekten, die ihre Aufgabe hauptsächlich darin sehen, Raum zu organisieren und für die vorgesehenen oder wünschenswerten Nutzungen bereitzustellen. Manche kümmern sich außerdem um die künstlerische Aussage und um die Atmosphäre. Gert Wingårdh hat noch ein weiteres Anliegen. Für ihn hängen die Erscheinungsform und die Erlebnisqualität maßgeblich von Material und Detail sowie der Verarbeitung ab. In der schwedischen Botschaft in Berlin zum Beispiel bereitet die wunderbare Holzarbeit an Wänden und Treppen des Foyers aus leuchtend warm-orange gebeiztem Birkenholz physisches Wohlbehagen. Beim jüngsten Neubau für AstraZeneca, dem Bürogebäude gleich neben dem Eingangsbauwerk, trägt die handwerkliche Perfektion zur überzeugenden Dignität des Gebäudes bei. Makellosigkeit kann eine Form der Schönheit sein und Wingårdh lässt sich nicht nachsagen, dass er die schönen Dinge des Lebens vernachlässige.

Immer wieder sieht sich Wingårdh durch Kunsterlebnisse inspiriert. Der schwedische Maler Marcus Larsson hat den Ausblick auf die Wildnis im sicheren Studio in Paris gemalt. Wingårdh übersetzt die Situation beim Zitadellenbad in Landskrona mit dem Blick durch schmale Schlitze aus dem domestizierten Bad auf das ungebändigte Meer. Und David Hockneys Poolbilder zitiert er mit dem Dekor der Bodenfliesen.

Den Laura Ashley Shop in Stockholm bezeichnet er als eine Collage aus *ready-mades* und bezieht sich auf Marcel Duchamp. Der Seitenblick auf die Arbeit

via the backdrop of the house. VillAnn opens out to the afternoon and evening sun across its full width like a stage, in order to capture the very last rays of sun—and allows passers-by on the shore road to participate in its vitality. The country estate Sand is a similar case—here, the fourth wall facing the sea is replaced by an unframed view. Villa Nilsson and the villa just outside Amundön celebrate the panorama in different ways—as an experience of architecture and of landscape. In Villa Astrid the visitor experiences a release into space after having entered the house through a narrow situation from above and having climbed down into the widening room.

One site-related theme that Gert Wingårdh enjoys taking up during his investigation into the topography of the site is that of developed rocky cliffs, which is encountered often enough on construction sites in Sweden's coastal regions. Wingårdh came into contact with his favoured local limestone at a young age, and was influenced by his games in the countryside, and by his father's factory. He views the landscape as a place to live: for him, man is archaically merged with the soil. His houses do not rise to distance themselves from the ground that they are built on—they nestle or even bury into it, becoming one with the place itself. Often, his houses fit into the rock formations, and the rocks even grow into the house, conveying the calming sense of being rooted in something to their inhabitants. In Villa Astrid or in Villa Nilsson the rocks penetrate into the house and "earth" it. At the Universeum in Göteborg, he was able to tackle this theme again, but on a larger scale. The building is built on the rock; an outsized glasshouse arches over the rocky rise, protecting the fauna and flora so that it can develop under tropical conditions.

Wherever there is a need to continue building artificially, he abstracts the rock with his own layers of stone. He piles up stone layers in the form of slabs and steps, which are not placed neatly one above the other in flights of steps, but rather—for example in Villa Nilsson—in an open arrangement, heightening a natural situation in an artistic way. The interior of Öijared Golf Club is an artistic interpretation of the rocky landscape. The open steps in front of the villa near Amundön appear more geometric. But even the setting of a single, simple step at Sand does not take place without appropriate consideration. Here and there, there are reminders of Carlo Scarpa, who is also one of Wingårdh's favourites. There are architects who see their primary task as organising space and preparing it for projected or desirable uses. Some also pay attention to the artistic message and atmosphere. Gert Wingårdh has a further objective; as he sees it, architecture as a manifestation and quality of experience is definitively dependent on materials and details, as well as the way that these are handled. In the Swedish embassy in Berlin, for example, the wonderful woodwork on the walls and steps of the foyer—in glowing, warm orange birch wood—creates physical wellbeing. The perfect craftsmanship of his latest new building for AstraZeneca, the office building next to the reception building, contributes to its convincing dignity. Flawlessness can be a form of beauty and Wingårdh will not let it be said of him that he neglects the beautiful things in life.

Repeatedly, Wingårdh sees himself inspired by his experience of art. The Swedish painter Marcus Larsson painted views out into the wilderness from the safety of his Paris studio. At the Zitadellenbad swimming pool in Landskrona, Wingårdh translates this situation into a view through narrow slits from the domesticated pool to the unrestrained sea. And he cites David Hockney's pool pictures with the decor of the floor tiles.

He describes his Laura Ashley shop in Stockholm as a collage of *ready-mades*, so referring to Marcel Duchamp. This side-glance at that artist's work is certainly justified, since a desire for artistic expression is one of the essential driving forces behind Wingårdh's own work.

Having already emphasised sustainability in his early works, he has since become known as an ecologically oriented architect, although he has never quite been a fanatical ecological activist. Öijared,

der Künstler ist sicherlich dadurch begründet, dass der Wille zum künstlerischen Ausdruck eine der wesentlichen Antriebsfedern für Wingårdhs Arbeit selbst darstellt.

Doch man kennt ihn durchaus auch als ökologisch orientierten Architekten, wenngleich er nie zum fanatisch kämpfenden Öko-Aktivisten geworden ist. Schon früh hat er bei seinen Bauten auf Nachhaltigkeit Wert gelegt. Öijared, Ale, Chalmers und Universeum sind ökologische Leitbauten und Sony Ericsson in Lund wurde als erste Hauptverwaltung in Schweden als „Green Building" deklariert.

Manchmal will Wingårdh sich selbst ausdrücken und nicht die Welt verändern. So ist auch sein Enga-

Noch stößt er mit seinen Ideen auf taube Ohren. Der Typus Hochhaus, für ihn genuines städtebauliches Element wahrhaft großer Städte, gilt als unschwedisch und so wird es wohl noch länger bei dem einzigen Beispiel von Calatravas Turning Torso in Malmö bleiben. Und auch für Wingårdh bleibt damit der Bau eines Hochhauses die große Herausforderung, das noch offene Thema.

Eine weitere Herausforderung ist die Internationalisierung, die Expansion ins Ausland, die für Wingårdh nach der Jahrtausendwende mit ersten Projekten in Skandinavien begann. Bald standen auch die USA, England, Deutschland, Frankreich und Russland auf der Agenda.

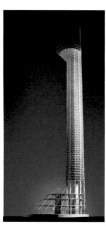

SERGELS TOWER, STOCKHOLM (SE), RENDERING SERGELS TOWER, STOCKHOLM (SE), RENDERING SCANDINAVIAN TOWER, MALMÖ (SE) SCANDINAVIAN TOWER, MALMÖ (SE) VICTORIA TOWER, KISTA (SE), RENDERING VICTORIA TOWER, KISTA (SE) RENDERING MALMÖ ARENA, MALMÖ (SE) MALMÖ ARENA, MALMÖ (SE)

gement für (im Grunde genommen unökologische) Hochhäuser zu verstehen, die er für Göteborg und Stockholm geplant hat. Schon 1980 hatte er, geboren aus seiner Begeisterung für Manhattan, für das Südufer in Göteborg Hochhäuser vorgeschlagen. Ein 274 Meter hohes Büro- und Wohnhaus – „Scandinavian Tower" – sollte in Malmö-Hyllie emporwachsen. Auch für Stockholm hat er Hochhauspläne in der Schublade. Am Stadtplatz Sergels Torg sollte der elegante Sergel Tower mit Wohnungen mehr internationales Fluidum in die Stadt bringen. In Göteborg am Heden sollten es gleich vier Hochhäuser sein, die auf Wallgraben und Innenstadt blicken.

366 Projekte listet das Werkverzeichnis des Architekten auf, das im Buch *Thirty years of architecture through four decades* abgedruckt ist, einschließlich 152 Wettbewerbsarbeiten und 52 siegreicher Projekte. Das von Kurator Mikael Nanfeldt herausgegebene Buch erschien im Zusammenhang mit einer Ausstellung im Röhsska Museum of Design, Fashion and Decorative Arts in Göteborg, in der Wingårdh im Winter 2007–08 „Åtta hus" präsentierte, seine acht Lieblingshäuser, danach noch um drei Häuser erweitert als „Elva hus", zu sehen in Stockholm, Helsinki und an anderen Orten. Die Liste mag nicht vollständig sein, doch sie zeigt vor allem eine beein-

Ale, Chalmers and the Universeum are pioneering constructions in ecological terms and Sony Ericsson in Lund was the first administrative headquarters in Sweden to be declared a "green building". Sometimes Wingårdh would like to express himself rather than attempting to change the world. It is in this context that one should see his commitment to the (basically non-ecological) high-rise buildings that he has planned for Göteborg and Stockholm. Borne of his enthusiasm for Manhattan, he had suggested high-rises for the south bank in Göteborg as early as 1980. His intention was for a 274-metre-high office and residential building—the "Scandinavian Tower"—to rise above Malmö-Hyllie.

of a high-rise remains the great challenge, an issue that remains open.

Another challenge is internationalisation, an expansion abroad which began with his first projects in the rest of Scandinavia in the new millennium. Soon the USA, England, Germany, France and Russia joined the agenda.

366 projects are listed in the catalogue of works printed in the publication *Thirty years of architecture through four decades*, including 152 works for competitions and 52 winning projects. Edited by curator Mikael Nanfeldt, this book appeared in connection with an exhibition in the Röhsska Museum of Design, Fashion and Decorative Arts in Göte-

KLINIK KAROLINSKA, SOLNA (SE), RENDERING HOSPITAL KAROLINSKA, SOLNA (SE), RENDERING SKULPTURENMUSEUM GLASKASTEN, MARL (DE), RENDERING MUSEUM OF SCULPTURE'S "GLASS BOX", MARL (DE), RENDERING MÜRITZEUM, WAREN/MÜRITZ (DE) MÜRITZEUM, WAREN/MÜRITZ (DE)

He also has various high-rise plans for Stockholm tucked away in a drawer. On the city square Sergels Torg, his idea for the elegant Sergel Tower of apartments was to create more of an international aura in the city. On Heden in Göteborg, he planned a total of four high-rises with views down to the historic moat and inner city. But his ideas fall on deaf ears, even today. The high-rise, which he sees as a genuine urban-developmental element of truly big cities, is regarded as un-Swedish—and it will probably remain so for a long time, notwithstanding the isolated example of Calatrava's Turning Torso in Malmö. For Wingårdh, therefore, the construction

borg, where Wingårdh presented "Åtta hus" in winter 2007–08: a presentation of his eight favourite houses, subsequently extended by three to "Elva hus" and shown in Stockholm, Helsinki and other venues. The list may not be complete, but above all it shows the office's impressive, constantly increasing productivity in the last years before the recession, with an annual increase in working hours of ten to 14 per cent.

The assignments are getting bigger; now they include urban-developmental projects like that for Copenhagen, the Maritima Center Göteborg in 2003, a hospital for Solna, or a multifunctional centre at the

druckende, in den letzten Jahren vor der Rezession ständig steigende Produktivität des Büros mit einer Zunahme der Arbeitsstunden um jährlich stattliche zehn bis 14 Prozent.

Und die Aufgaben werden größer, mittlerweile sind auch städtebauliche Entwürfe wie jener für Kopenhagen darunter, das Maritima Center Göteborg 2003, ein Krankenhaus für Solna oder ein multifunktionales Zentrum am Oslo Terminal für Helsingborg 2005. Doch immer noch reizen Wingårdh die kleinen Arbeiten, die Feriendomizile, die Villen und Einfamilienhäuser. Für Arkitekthus entwarf er 2004 drei Kataloghäuser, von denen rund drei Dutzend gebaut wurden.

machte sich hier seine Erfahrungen zunutze, die er acht Jahre zuvor beim Bau des Ale Kulturzentrums und des Gymnasiums in Nödinge just am gegenüberliegenden Ufer des Göta älv gesammelt hatte. Verschiedene Schulen, Erwachsenenbildung, Musikschule, Theater und Bibliothek wurden in einem integralen Verbund organisiert. Die helle und großzügige Architektur unterstützt das Prinzip des offenen Hauses, das keine räumliche Trennung zwischen Schule und öffentlichen Nutzungen kennt. Das übersichtliche Erschließungssystem der umfangreichen, in vier miteinander verbundene Einzelbaukörper gegliederten Anlage stellt auch Neuankömmlinge nicht vor unüberwindliche Orientierungsprobleme.

WOHNHAUS NORRA DJURGÅRDSSTADEN, STOCKHOLM (SE), RENDERING RESIDENTIAL BUILDING NORRA DJURGÅRDSSTADEN, STOCKHOLM (SE), RENDERING KUGGEN, MALMÖ (SE), RENDERING KUGGEN, MALMÖ (SE), RENDERING BESUCHERZENTRUM, LAPONIA (SE), RENDERING VISITOR CENTRE, LAPONIA (SE), RENDERING

Wie immer im Architektenleben wurde viel Fantasie und Arbeit umsonst investiert, kam die Mehrzahl der Entwürfe über das Wettbewerbs- oder Projektstadium nicht hinaus. Dennoch können sich die Ausführungs- und Detailplaner und die Baumanager im Büro über Mangel an Arbeit nicht beklagen. Das 2000 eröffnete, elegant geschwungene Allgon Bürozentrum in Rönninge Täby am Anfang des Großraums Stockholm liegt nahe der E18 Richtung Norrtälje und der Fähre nach Finnland. An der E6 von Göteborg nach Norden liegt Kungälv. Dort entstand das Bildungs- und Kulturzentrum Mimers Hus mit einer ganz neuen funktionalen Konzeption. Wingårdh

In Kungsbacka südlich von Göteborg entstand die jüngste Schule des Büros. Dabei ging es um den Umbau und die Erweiterung des Aranäsgymnasiums aus den sechziger Jahren. Wieder ist es ein ganz neuer Entwurf, der sich intensiv auf die vorgefundene Situation einlässt. Nur der an Ale erinnernde Grundriss der Neubautrakte lässt an Wingårdh als den Architekten denken – und natürlich der unvermeidliche Kalkstein. Auch bei der Fassadengestaltung des Schauspielhauses mit 500 Plätzen erprobte Wingårdh eine neue Ästhetik. „TEATER" schrieb er in riesigen Metalllettern an die schwarze Betonfertigteilwand, wie es vielleicht Venturi auch

Oslo Terminal to Helsingborg in 2005. But he is still attracted by small works—such as holiday homes, villas and detached family houses. He also designed three catalogue houses for Arkitekthus in 2004, around three dozen of which have been built.

As always in any architect's life, a lot of imagination and work has been invested for nothing—the majority of designs got no further than the competition or project phase. Nevertheless, the realisation- and detail-planners and the construction managers in the office cannot complain that they do not have enough work to do.

Opened in 2000, the elegantly curving Allgon office centre in Rönninge Täby on the edge of the metro-

tial separation between school and public uses. The clear system of access in the extensive complex—which is divided into four connected but individual volumes—presents no insurmountable problems of orientation even for new arrivals.

The office's most recent school project was realised in Kungsbacka, south of Göteborg. It concerned the conversion and extension of Aranäs Grammar School, which dates from the sixties. Again, it is a brand new design that demonstrates an intense involvement in the existing situation. Only the ground plan of the new wings, reminiscent of Ale, suggests Wingårdh as the architect—as of course does the inevitable limestone. For the façade design of

SVEN-HARRY KARLSSON MUSEUM, STOCKHOLM (SE), RENDERING SVEN-HARRY KARLSSON MUSEUM, STOCKHOLM (SE), RENDERING ARANÄSGYMNASIUM, KUNGSBACKA (SE) ARANÄS GRAMMAR SCHOOL, KUNGSBACKA (SE) BÜROBAU ALLGON, RÖNNINGE TÄBY (SE) HALLE UND SÜDANSICHT OFFICE BUILDING ALLGON, RÖNNINGE TÄBY (SE) HALL AND SOUTH ELEVATION

politan area of Stockholm is close to the E18 heading towards Norrtälje and the ferry to Finland. Kungälv is located on the E6 from Göteborg to the north. Here, Wingårdh created the educational and cultural centre Mimers Hus, employing a new functional concept. He made use of experience collected eight years before during the construction of the Ale Cultural Centre and the Grammar School in Nödinge on the opposite bank of the Göta älv. Various schools, an adult education centre, a music school, a theatre and a library have been combined into an integral complex. The bright, expansive architecture is based on the open-house principle, creating no spa-

the theatre with 500 seats, Wingårdh also experimented with new aesthetics. He wrote "TEATER" in huge metal letters on the black wall of prefabricated concrete panels, as Venturi would perhaps have done. The project was awarded the Kasper Salin Prize 2006.

In addition to the Müritzeum, Wingårdh will soon be building another museum in Germany. In 2005 he won the competition for the Museum of Sculpture's "glass box" in Marl, a town in the Ruhr area. His design for the extension of the old museum—built to relate to the town hall by the Rotterdam architects van den Broek and Bakema in 1962–66—envis-

getan hätte. Das Projekt wurde mit dem Kasper Salin Preis 2006 ausgezeichnet.

Neben dem Müritzeum wird er ein weiteres Museum in Deutschland bauen. Er gewann 2005 den Wettbewerb für das Skulpturenmuseum Glaskasten in der Ruhrgebietsstadt Marl. Sein Entwurf für die Erweiterung des 1962–66 von den Rotterdamer Architekten van den Broek und Bakema im räumlichen Zusammenhang mit dem Rathaus gebauten Museums sieht einen 85 Meter langen balkenartigen, über den benachbarten Teich auskragenden Schauraum vor. Am Ende des langen, durch Oberlichte erhellten Raums wartet wieder die Überraschung: der freie Ausblick nach Süden über Teich und Stadt.

2007 gewann Wingårdh den Wettbewerb für das neue Zentrum in Mölndal. Die Bebauung mit Geschäften, Wohnhäusern und öffentlichen Nutzungen schließt unmittelbar westlich an den Knotenpunkt an, den er gebaut hat, wodurch sich eine gestalterische Verbindung ergibt. Ein vierzig-geschossiges Hochhaus soll das neue Zentrum akzentuieren. Noch ist offen, ob es ihm dieses Mal gelingt, ein Hochhausprojekt zu realisieren.

Besonders ausgeprägte architektonische Aussagen lassen sich immer mit Museumsbauten machen, so auch bei den zwei jüngsten Museumsprojekten. Am Stockholmer Vasapark entsteht das Sven-Harry Karlsson Museum als „Messingkästchen" mit wertvollem Inhalt und Beispiel für ein vertikal organisiertes Museum mit unterschiedlichen Funktionen. Über den kommerziellen Galerien im Erdgeschoss liegt die öffentliche Kunsthalle. Die Privatsammlung des Stifters ist im Penthouse ausgestellt. Die Kosten werden durch Vermietung von zwölf Apartments bestritten. Die golden schimmernde Fassade besteht aus einer neuen Legierung aus Kupfer, Aluminium, Zink und Zinn, die unter Wettereinfluss nicht nachdunkelt.

Eine sehr naturnahe Fassade dagegen erhält Snöfällan, ein Besucherzentrum in Lappland, in dem die Kultur der Samen zu erleben ist. Mit seiner Außenwand aus gestapelten Hölzern und seiner runden Form fügt es sich in die urtümliche Landschaft ein und vermittelt auf sinnliche Weise ein intensives Gefühl für die Lebenswelt der Samen. Um das zentrale Atrium sind Ausstellungsräume, Auditorium, Café und Serviceräume angeordnet.

Auch für die Technische Universität Chalmers in Göteborg ist Wingårdh wieder tätig geworden. Auf dem Campus, der sich auf dem ehemaligen Werftgelände Lindholm entwickelt hat, baut Wingårdh ein Kommunikations- und Bürozentrum für Wissenschaftler, der Grundrissform wegen „Kuggen" (Zahnrad) genannt, das in höchstem Maße nachhaltig sein soll. Es wird mit Fotovoltaik, thermischer Solarnutzung und einem hocheffizienten Energiemanagement ausgestattet und ist für eine lange Lebenszeit konzipiert. Mit seiner Rundform, der leuchtend roten Schuppenfassade und den Dreiecksfenstern ist es für den Campus ein Wahrzeichen mit hohem Wiedererkennungswert.

Wingårdhs Bekanntheitsgrad steht noch immer hinter seiner Bedeutung zurück. Das hat wohl damit zu tun, dass er in keine Schublade zu passen scheint und man ihm kein Label anheften kann. Seine formale, immer an der Aufgabe orientierte Vielfalt verhindert die Entstehung eines Individualstils oder einer wiedererkennbaren Handschrift; dies entspricht nicht der Erwartungshaltung des Publikums und der Expertenschaft. Auch beteiligt er sich an keinen Theoriedebatten und liefert keine Erklärungen und Interpretationen seiner Werke. Andererseits gibt ihm das die erwünschten Spielräume. Weil er nicht theoretisiert, ist er frei zu tun, was ihm gerade einfällt. Wingårdh trägt keinen moralischen Imperativ vor sich her und fühlt sich keiner Ideologie verpflichtet. Er muss sich nicht an seinen eigenen Manifestationen messen lassen. Mit einer gewissen Leichtigkeit des Seins geht er die Dinge immer neu an, immer wach, immer reaktionsfreudig. Wie kaum ein zweiter schwedischer Architekt reagiert er geschmeidig auf die Klienten, hört ihnen zu, realisiert ihre Wünsche – um dann doch daraus seine eigene Architektur zu formen, seine Qualitätsansprüche durchzusetzen und mit jeder Aufgabe das zu realisieren, was ihm am Herzen liegt: Architektur, die mit allen Sinnen zu erleben ist.

ages an 85-metre-long, shaft-like exhibition space projecting over the adjacent pond. At the end of this long space lit by skylights, another surprise lies in wait for visitors: an open view across the pond and the city to the south.

In 2007 Wingårdh won the competition for the new centre in Mölndal. The development with shops, residential buildings and public uses begins immediately west of a junction that he himself conceived—and a design link emerges as a result. His project envisages a forty-storey high-rise to accentuate the new centre. It is still not clear whether he will finally succeed in realising a high-rise project this time.

Museum buildings are ideal for making outstanding architectonic statements, and this is also the case with Wingårdh's two most recent museum projects. By the Vasapark in Stockholm, the Sven-Harry Karlsson Museum is being created as a "brass box containing treasure" and is one example of a vertically laid-out museum with various functions. Above the commercial galleries on the ground floor one finds the public art gallery. The donor's private collection is exhibited in the penthouse. The costs will be met by renting out twelve apartments. The golden, shimmering façade consists of a new alloy of copper, aluminium, zinc, and tin, which will not darken as a result of weathering.

By contrast, a façade very close to nature will be provided for Snöfällan, a visitor centre in Lapland where it is possible to experience the Sami culture. Its exterior walls of stacked timbers and its round form mean that it fits into the original landscape and conveys an intense feel for the lifestyle and homeland of the Sami in a sensual way. Exhibition rooms, auditorium, café and service areas are set around a central atrium.

Wingårdh has also worked for Chalmers Technical University in Göteborg once again. On the campus that has developed on the former dockyard site of Lindholm, Wingårdh is building a communications and office centre for scientists, known as the "Kuggen" (cog) because of the shape of its ground plan. The building is envisioned to be extremely sustainable. It will be equipped with photovoltaics, thermal solar usage and highly efficient energy management; it is conceived for a long life. Its round form, bright-red scaled façade and triangular windows make it into a landmark for the campus that is easily recognisable. Wingårdh's reputation has not yet caught up with his significance as an architect. This may have something to do with the fact that he does not seem to fit into any category, and it is difficult to pin a label on him. His formal diversity, always oriented to the task in hand, has so far prevented the development of an individual style or a recognisable signature, whereas the public—and even experts in the field—tend to expect this. Nor does he participate at all in theoretical debates and provides no explanations or interpretations of his works. This gives him the freedom he desires: because he does not theorise, he is free to do whatever occurs to him at any one time. Wingårdh labours under no moral imperative and does not feel bound to any ideology. He has no need to measure himself against the manifestations of his own work.

He always sets about things in a new way, with a certain "lightness of being", always alert and ready to react. Very few other Swedish architects react so flexibly to clients, listening to them and realising their wishes; in order to create his own architecture from those wishes, he asserts his demands for quality and realises what is close to his heart with every task: architecture to experience with all the senses.

PROJEKTE
PROJECTS

Müritzeum, Waren (DE)

Waren an der Müritz, eine kleinen Stadt in der Mecklenburgischen Seenplatte, etwa auf halber Strecke zwischen Berlin und Kiel gelegen, ist ein beliebtes Wassersportzentrum mit einem herausgeputzten mittelalterlichen Stadtkern und idyllischem Freizeithafen.

Das Naturhistorische Museum der Stadt, untergebracht in einem denkmalgeschützten Schulbau aus dem Jahr 1860, war bislang ein verstaubtes Museum mit altväterlicher Didaktik, das zum attraktiven „Naturerlebniszentrum" aufgewertet werden sollte. Unmittelbar hinter dem Haus liegt der kleine Herrensee; dort fand sich der wegen seiner Naturnähe geeignete Platz für einen Neubau.

„Müritzeum" sollte der Neubau heißen. Gert Wingårdh, der den Wettbewerb für sich entscheiden konnte, nutzte die topografische Situation, indem er den Neubau an der Nordseite ins Wasser des Herrensees verschob und an der Südseite ein repräsentatives Vorfeld mit Blick und Verbindung zum Müritzufer schuf. Die Grundform des signifikanten Baukörpers, ein sich nach oben erweiternder Konus, macht den Bau zum Solitär, der sich mit seiner besonderen Nutzung als Blickfang präsentiert. Die Südseite des Gebäudes ist eine einzige weite Öffnung, eine große einladende Geste, die das Publikum anlockt und Schwellenangst nicht aufkommen lässt. Ein Großteil der Front wird vom Restaurant eingenommen, das mit Sonnenschirmen und Tischen im Freien ohnehin einladend wirkt. Links des Haupteingangs wendet sich der Museumsshop an die Passanten. Über dem Eingang macht das Vexierspiel des Schriftzugs „Müritzeum" neugierig, denn wie die fünffach hintereinander liegenden hölzernen Buchstaben montiert sind, wird nur aus der Nähe verständlich – und schon ist man halb eingetreten.

Von außen lässt das Museum alle Fotografen verzweifeln, da die tiefschwarze Fassade alles Licht verschluckt. Die aufgehenden Wände sind mit abgeflämmtem Brettholz mit verkohlter Oberfläche verkleidet. Nur die Partien in Reichweite der Nutzer und Besucher sind schwarz lackiert, um verschmutzte Kleidung zu vermeiden. Wingårdh war einmal an einer angebrannten Scheune die Dauerhaftigkeit des Materials aufgefallen, denn der Brand hatte 1927 stattgefunden!

Waren on the Müritz a small town located in the Mecklenburg Lakelands about half way between Berlin and Kiel is a popular water sports centre with a refurbished mediaeval town centre and an idyllic harbour.

The town's natural history museum, a rather dusty collection with old-fashioned didactics, had been accommodated previously in a listed school building from 1860. The intention was to improve and enhance this museum and so create an attractive "nature experience centre". Directly behind the school there is a small lake called the Herrensee, and this site's closeness to nature made it appropriate for the new building.

The centre was to be called the "Müritzeum". Gert Wingårdh succeeded in winning the competition for its design, and exploited the topographic situation to make the new building's north front project over the water of the Herrensee, while creating a representative approach with a view and connecting path to the bank of the Müritz in the south. The basic form of the significant architectural volume—a cone widening towards the top—makes the eye-catching structure with its special function quite unique. The south side of the building is a single wide opening: an expansive, welcoming gesture that attracts the public without allowing any fear of the unfamiliar to arise. A large part of the front is taken up by the restaurant, which is inviting in its own right, with a number of sunshades and tables in the open air. To the left of the main entrance, the museum shop attracts passers-by. Above the entrance, the puzzling written sign "Müritzeum" triggers curiosity, for the letters—placed one in front of the other five times—are only legible from close up. Before you know where you are, therefore, you are half inside.

From the outside, the museum drives every photographer to despair, because the black façade absorbs all the light. The walls are clad in flame-treated wooden boards with a charred surface. Only those areas within reach of the users and visitors have been varnished black to prevent their clothes becoming soiled. Wingårdh had realised the durability of the material after having seen a barn that had been burnt down; the fire had taken place as long ago as 1927!

Die Innenseite der schwarzen Schale, etwa das Interieur des Foyers und des Restaurants, ist dagegen in einem angenehmen, warmgoldenen Holzton gehalten. Die zwei Ausstellungsebenen sind aus museumstechnischen Gründen in Dunkelräume unterteilt, wobei sich die Kreisform des Hauses auch im Forum, einem Zentrum mit einführender Videoinstallation, und Themenräumen wiederfindet.

An einer Stelle des Rundgangs, im „Vogelsaal", öffnet sich die Fassade und der Besucher kann in eine Glaskanzel hinaustreten, die über das Wasser ragt. Im Untergeschoss erwecken zwei Aquarien mit Verbindung nach außen den Eindruck, als ob man unter die Wasseroberfläche des Sees blicken würde. Am Ende des Rundgangs führt ein Weg zum Lehrpfad rund um den Herrensee oder hinüber zum Altbau, wo es die naturhistorischen Sammlungen zu sehen gibt.

Hat man den kleinen See umrundet, erlebt man das Museum nochmals als schwarze Arche, die am Ufer liegt und sich im Wasser spie-

The inner surface of the black shell, including the interior of the foyer and the restaurant, is presented in a contrasting, pleasant warm-golden wood tone. In-house requirements mean that the two exhibition levels must be divided into dark rooms—the circular form of the building is echoed in the forum, for example, which is a centre including an introductory video installation and other thematic areas.

At one point in the tour—the "Bird Room"—the façade opens and the visitor can walk out onto a glass chancel projecting over the water. On the basement floor, two aquaria with a connection to the outside give visitors the impression that they can see beneath the lake's surface. At the end of the tour a path leads either onto the nature trail around the Herrensee or across to the old building, where it is possible to view the natural history collections.

Having walked around the small lake, one perceives the museum once again—as a black ark moored by the shore and reflected in

gelt. Ein Steg führt wieder hinüber zum Museum, aber auch zur Außentreppe, die sich schräg an der überhängenden Wand hinaufwindet und den Gleichgewichtssinn auf die Probe stellt. Oben auf der Dachterrasse genießt man einen wunderbaren Blick hinüber zur Altstadt und über die glitzernde Fläche der Müritz.

Mit der ungewöhnlichen Form des Müritzeums weckt der Architekt Assoziationen an Schiffe, an Kähne, an die tausend Seen der Mecklenburgischen Seenplatte. Er tut dies mit einer modernen Architektursprache ganz subtil auf abstrahierende Weise ohne Rückgriff auf gängige Typologien und erzeugt eine dem Ort und dem Thema angemessene Atmosphäre, ohne plakative oder gar kitschige formale Mittel einsetzen zu müssen. Mit den Fassaden und Wänden aus verkohltem und frischem Holz verbindet sich das Haus harmonisch mit seiner natürlichen Umgebung und greift Themen auf, die in einem Naturkundemuseum, das von Moor- und Heidelandschaften handelt, eine entscheidende Rolle spielen.

the water. A pier leads back to the museum, but also to the external staircase twisting obliquely up the overhanging wall and testing the visitor's sense of balance. Having reached the roof terrace there is a wonderful view across the old town and the huge glittering expanse of the Müritz.

The architect exploits the Müritzeum's unusual form to awaken associations with ships, barges, and the thousand lakes of Mecklenburg's lakeland area. He does so with a modern architectural language that is subtle and abstracting, without adopting commonplace typologies: he creates an atmosphere suited to the place and its theme without the need to apply over-simplified or even kitschy formal means. The façades and walls made of flame-treated and fresh wood enable the building to enter into a harmonious union with its natural environment and to echo themes that play a decisive role for any museum of natural history focusing on marsh- and moorland landscapes.

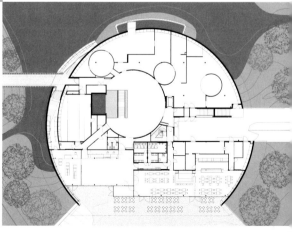

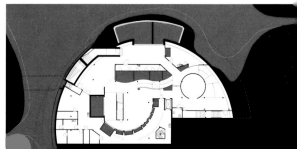

Öijared Executive Country Club, Lerum (SE)

Dreißig Kilometer östlich von Göteborg an der E20 Richtung Stockholm geht es links ab, die Allee auf das klassizistische Schlösschen Nääs zu, dann noch fünf Kilometer in die Wälder, bis die Golfplätze ins Blickfeld geraten. Man folgt dem Weg vom Parkplatz durch den Birkenhain, plötzlich tut sich die Erde auf und gibt eine gläserne Eingangsfront frei. Noch ist das Ausmaß des Gebäudes nicht zu erkennen. Man umrundet den Hügel und steht vor der Südwestfront, wo die Fassaden tanzen, wo die Pfosten und Glaswände vor- und zurückspringen, als seien Glashäute zwischen die Birkenstämme gespannt. Der Landschaftsraum fließt fast ungehindert ins Innere. Ein hölzerner Sonnenschirm säumt die Traufe, schließt die Glasfront nach oben ab und dient gleichzeitig als „horizontaler Zaun" zum Schutz der Golfer auf dem Dach.

Denn manchmal stehen zwei Spieler auf dem Klubhaus und diskutieren den nächsten Schlag. Das Grasdach des Golfklubs steigt sanft aus der Landschaft des Golfplatzes und senkt sich wieder herab, da kann man eben auch vom Dach aus den Abschlag spielen. Der amerikanische Architekt Emilio Ambasz hatte mit seinen zum Teil mit Erde überdeckten Bauten die Vorbilder geliefert, wenngleich nicht in dieser Konsequenz. Gert Wingårdh begibt sich ganz in den Schutz der Erde und öffnet nur den Ausblick in die Landschaft. Das Haus ist buchstäblich in die Natur hineingebaut.

Der Naturraum setzt sich im Inneren fort, wo er terrassenförmig über sechs Ebenen vom Golfsportgeschäft zur Rechten und den Klubräumen zur Linken des Eingangs bis zu den Sitzungsräumen ansteigt. Eine Vielzahl von Aufenthalts- und Sitzmöglichkeiten unterschiedlichen Charakters mit bequemen Sofas stehen zur Auswahl. Besonders hervorgehoben auf der mittleren Ebene der Kaminplatz, der mit seinen Wänden und dem Schornstein aus grob geschichtetem Naturstein an Frank Lloyd Wrights Präriehäuser erinnert. Noch etwas höher liegt das Restaurant mit dem besten Überblick nach

Thirty kilometres east of Göteborg on the E20 to Stockholm one turns off to the left, drives along the road towards the small classical manor of Nääs, and then continues for five kilometres through woodland until it is possible to catch sight of the golf courses. After following a path from the car park through a copse of birch trees, the earth suddenly opens up to reveal a glass front and entrance. It is still impossible to see the extent of the building. Walking around the hillock one finds oneself standing in front of the south-west front, where the façades dance, the posts and glazed walls skipping backwards and forwards as if glass membranes had been stretched between the birch trees. The landscape flows almost unhindered into the building's interior.

A wooden shade against the sun edges the eaves, terminating the glazed front at the top and simultaneously functioning as a "horizontal fence" to protect the golfers on the roof, for two players will sometimes stand on top of the club house discussing their next shot. The golf club's grass roof rises gently from the landscape of the golf course and slopes back down again, making it possible to tee off from the roof. The American architect Emilio Ambasz provided the model, with his buildings insulated by earth—although they were only partially covered. Gert Wingårdh is more consistent, burying the structure completely in the ground and opening out no more than a view into the landscape. The clubhouse is literally built into nature.

The natural sphere continues inside, where—like a terrace—it rises through six levels, from the golf shop to the right and the clubrooms to the left of the entrance area, to the conference areas. There are many places to sit and linger, varied in character, but all with comfortable sofas. The fireplace area on the middle level is particularly accentuated; its walls and chimney-piece of rough natural stone make it reminiscent of Frank Lloyd Wright's prairie houses. A

innen und außen. Wieder einige Stufen tiefer daran anschließend der Executive Club, der wiederum mit den rückwärtigen Sitzungsräumen in Verbindung steht und einen Blick hinab ins Schwimmbad erlaubt. Die Deckenhöhe steigt von zwei Metern über den niedrigen Klubräumen auf bis zu sieben Meter über dem Schwimmbad.

Dem gesamten Bau liegt ein Dreieckskonstruktionsraster zugrunde. Es entstehen kristalline Formen, die mit den geologischen Strukturen der Landschaft und des Hügels korrespondieren. Bodenbeläge, Treppen und Wände aus örtlichem roten Kalkstein verstärken den Effekt des sich höhlenartig in den anstehenden Felsen schmiegenden Raums. Stützen und Fensterpfosten hingegen scheinen die

little higher up there is the restaurant with the best view across the interior and exterior. Abutting this and only a few steps down is the Executive Club, which is connected in turn to the conference rooms at the back and provides a view down into the swimming pool. The height of the ceilings increases from two metres above the low clubrooms to seven metres above the swimming pool.

The whole building is based on a triangular construction grid. As a consequence, crystalline forms evolve and correspond to the geological structures of the landscape and hill. Floors, steps, and walls made of local red limestone heighten the impression of a space nestling into the adjacent hillside like a cave. By contrast,

außenstehenden Birkenstämme zu wiederholen. So gehen Architektur und Natur eine enge Verbindung ein.

Ein Nebengang führt ins Geschoss auf der unteren Ebene, wo vier Saunen auf die Gäste warten, sowie der Pool, der wie ein Bergsee halb in den Hang gegraben ist und auf der anderen Seite einen Blick ins Grüne bietet.

Bei Sommersonne ist der Klub ein angenehm kühler Aufenthaltsort, von dem aus das sportliche Treiben draußen auf dem Grün entspannt beobachtet werden kann. Bei ungemütlichem Wetter lässt es sich in dieser warmen, geschützten Atmosphäre entspannt plaudern und feiern.

Der Golfklub versöhnt sich mit der Natur: Er versucht, sich organisch einzufügen und die Natur so wenig wie möglich zu beeinträchtigen. Auch wärmetechnisch hat das Haus engen Kontakt mit Natur und Landschaft, denn es bezieht den Großteil seiner Energie aus geothermischen Bohrungen in der Erde. Zusammen mit dem Effekt der Erddeckung ergab sich ein für die späten achtziger Jahre bemerkenswertes Energieeinsparungspotenzial von 40 Prozent. Ein nachhaltiges, ein frühes Ökohaus also für eine Klientel, die damals in solchen Kategorien sicher noch nicht denken wollte. Gert Wingårdh erhielt dafür 1988 seinen ersten Kasper Salin Preis.

the structural supports and window posts seem to echo the birch trees standing outside. Thus the architecture and nature enter into a close symbiosis.

An auxiliary entrance opens onto the lowest floor level, where four saunas await guests, as well as the pool, which is half-buried in the slope like a mountain lake and offers a view across the green landscape on the other side.

In the summer sun, the club is a pleasantly cool place to linger—ideal for relaxing and watching the sport being played outside on the green. When the weather is less cosy, it is possible to chat and celebrate at ease in this warm and sheltered atmosphere.

The golf club is reconciled with nature: it seeks to fit in organically and encroach on nature as little as possible. The house is also closely bound to the landscape with respect to heating and ventilation technology—geothermic boreholes in the ground are the source of most of its energy. Together with the covering of earth, this results in an energy saving potential of 40 per cent, which was quite remarkable for the late eighties. And so this is a sustainable, early ecological building for a clientele who had not yet begun to think in such categories at the time. Gert Wingårdh received his first Kasper Salin Prize for the project in 1988.

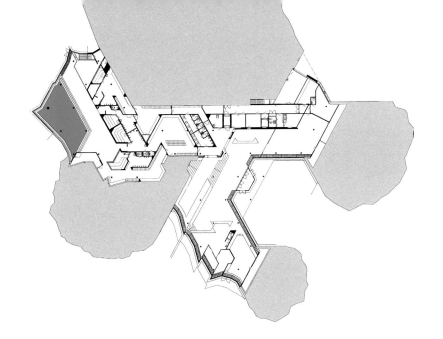

Villa bei Amundön, Skintebo (SE)
Villa near Amundön, Skintebo (SE)

Wingårdhs Lust an der dramaturgischen Inszenierung der Landschaft hat auch beim Entwurf dieser Villa die entscheidende Rolle gespielt. Denn das privilegierte Grundstück liegt an einem nach Westen orientierten Ufer einer Bucht mit weitem, freiem Blick auf die Insel Amundön und die Schären vor Billdal, der die Attraktion des Ortes ausmacht.

Wer sich dem Haus von der Straße her nähert, dem wird die traumhafte Aussicht noch vorenthalten. Ein schlichter Asphaltweg führt, flankiert von blanken Felsen, auf das Haus zu, von dem nur eine abweisend geschlossene Betonwand mit einem von einem Staketengatter geschlossenen Eingang und dem Garagentor zu sehen ist.

Doch wenn sich die Haustür öffnet, kommt im Hintergrund des

Wingårdh loves staging landscape in a dramatic way—a penchant that was also decisive in the design of this villa. The plot is most advantageous: located on the western-facing shore of a bay with a view of the Island of Amundön and the skerries off the coast of Billdal in the distance, all making the setting highly attractive.

However, the fantastic view is withheld from those approaching the villa from the road. A simple asphalt path flanked by bare rock leads towards the house, and all that can be seen initially is an unfriendly, unbroken concrete wall with a picket gated entrance and the garage door.

But as soon as the door to the house is opened, a very high window presenting a panorama of the bay can be seen at the back of the

Raums ein sehr hohes Fenster mit dem Panorama der Bucht ins Blickfeld. Das ganze Haus am Hang ist auf dieses Panorama ausgerichtet. Bei der zentralen Treppe hinab in den Wohnbereich, die den Ausblick zelebriert, bedient sich der Architekt illusionistischer Tricks der Renaissancearchitekten. Die Treppe verengt sich auf dem Weg nach unten, während das anschließende Wasserbecken vor dem Haus, das die Blickachse verlängert, sich nach draußen verbreitert und die Illusion der perspektivischen Verkürzung hervorruft. Die Fassade, die durch kalksteinerne Schotten in einzelne Fenster unterteilt ist, fächert sich auf und öffnet die Wohn- und Aufenthaltsräume und die vorgelagerte Terrasse ebenfalls in die Hauptblickrichtung Amundön.

room. The whole house on the slope is oriented towards this panorama: the architect makes use of an illusionary trick practised by renaissance architects for the central stairs down into the living area, which "celebrates" the view. The staircase narrows on the way down, while the pool of water directly in front of the house—which extends the viewing axis—widens outwards and creates the illusion of perspective foreshortening. Separated into individual windows by limestone partitions, the façade fans out and opens the living room, recreation rooms, and terrace in the main viewing direction towards Amundön.

This generates a brightly-lit zone and a darker area at the back of the space. The study, three children's rooms, and a playroom are

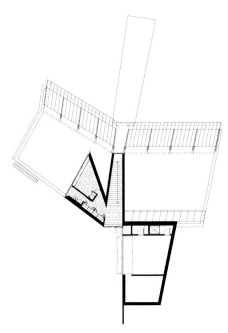

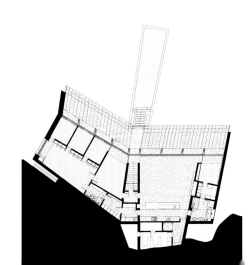

So entstehen eine hell belichtete Raumzone und ein dunklerer rückwärtiger Raum. Das Arbeitszimmer, drei Kinderzimmer und ein Spielzimmer liegen links der Treppe, der große Wohnraum und das Elternschlafzimmer zur Rechten. Die bergseitige Küchenzeile am Ende des Wohnraums wird durch einen Oberlichtstreifen in helles Zenitlicht getaucht. Hinter der Küche sind Vorratsräume in den Fels gesprengt und der Aufzug hinauf in die Garage angeordnet.

Wichtigster Baustoff ist das Sonnenlicht, das im Treppenschacht dramatische Effekte an die Wände wirft, das durch die Schotten in scharfe Rechtecke geschnitten wird, das am Abend Reflexe in den Raum wirft und nach der Dämmerung durch eine Kunstlichtinszenierung ersetzt wird. Dann strahlen die von innen erleuchteten Schotten wie Seezeichen über die Schären.

situated to the left of the stairs; the big living room and parents' bedroom is to the right. The fitted kitchen at the back of the living room is submerged in bright zenith light by an overhead strip-light. Behind the kitchen, storage areas have been blasted into the rocks; the lift up to the garage is also located here.

The most important building material is sunlight: it projects dramatic effects onto the walls in the stairwell. The sunlight is cut into sharp rectangles by the partitions, throwing reflections into the room in the evening, and is replaced after dusk by a staged scenario of artificial light. Then the partitions, lit from within, shine over the skerries like some kind of maritime signal.

Kajplats 01, Malmö (SE)

Viele Hafenstädte haben das Problem, aber auch die Chance, dass innenstadtnahe Hafengebiete nicht mehr benötigt werden und für Stadtentwicklungsmaßnahmen zur Verfügung stehen. In Malmö ist es der Västra Hamn (Westhafen) mit seiner exponierten Lage an der Wasserkante der Stadt. 2001 wurde auf dem city- und strandnahen Hafen- und Industriegelände im Rahmen der Bauausstellung Bo01 die „Stadt von morgen" präsentiert. Ein zukunftsweisendes, nachhaltiges Vorzeigeprojekt mit maximaler Wohnqualität wurde geplant, ohne Autoverkehr – der wurde ins Untergeschoss verbannt. Der Architekt Klas Tham hatte den Masterplan für die 560 Wohneinheiten und 6000 Arbeitsplätze geliefert. Mit dabei das bekannte, 190 Meter hohe spiralförmige Wohnhochhaus Turning Torso von Santiago Calatrava als städtebaulicher Akzent. Gert Wingårdh war einer der Architekten, die für die kommunale Wohnungsbaugesellschaft MKB auf der Grundlage dieses Plans die anspruchsvollen Wohnhäuser entwarfen.

Ökologisch hochwertig sollten die Häuser sein, aber auch architektonisch von erster Güte. Wingårdh hatte sich nicht mehr und nicht weniger vorgenommen, als Häuser zu bauen, die mehr als 100 Jahre überdauern. Dazu wählte er erprobte Materialien, robuste Technik und bemühte sich um flexible, möglichst unspezifische Grundrisse, die sich wechselnden Ansprüchen anpassen können.

Many ports face not only the problems but also the opportunities created by the redundancy of harbour areas close to the inner city, making them available for urban-developmental measures. In Malmö this applies to the Västra Hamn (west harbour) with its outstanding position on the water-edge of the city. In 2001 the "city of tomorrow" on the port and industrial site close to the city and beach was presented in the context of the building exhibition Bo01. Plans were for a sustainable, forward-looking, showcase project ensuring maximum quality of living with no motor traffic, which was banished underground. The architect Klas Tham provided a master plan for the 560 housing units and 6000 jobs. It included the famous 190-metre-high spiral shaped residential high-rise "Turning Torso" by Santiago Calatrava as an urban-developmental accent. Gert Wingårdh was one of the architects who designed high-quality residential buildings on the basis of this plan for the municipal housing construction association MKB.

The houses were to be ecologically outstanding, but the intention was to create architectural quality as well. Wingårdh was determined to build houses that would endure for more than a hundred years—no more and no less. With this in mind, he chose tried and trusted materials and robust technology, and made an effort to cre-

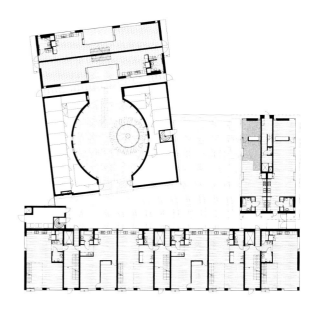

Um den rauen Winden zu begegnen, denen die Bebauung unmittelbar am Ufer des Öresunds fast ständig ausgesetzt ist, sah der Masterplan hohe, den Wind abschirmende Häuser an der Wasserfront und dahinter eine verwinkelte Bebauung mit vielen geschützten Ecken vor. Wingårdh nutzte die Möglichkeit der Kombination verschiedener Wohnungstypen und Hausbreiten, um einen Baukörper mit ungemein abwechslungsreichem und daher unverwechselbarem Gesicht zu schaffen. Hinzu kommen die diversen Fensterformate, mal quer gelagert, mal raumhoch, mal als stockwerkübergreifende zweigeschossige Verglasung, die einen großartigen Ausblick auf den Sund und die Öresundbrücke bietet. Wie eine geometrische Matrix wirkt die Hauptansicht und nur mit Mühe lassen sich die Geschosse ablesen. Auch die Verkleidung der unteren Fassadenzone mit Natursteinplatten gibt keinen Hinweis: Sie reicht bis zur Hälfte des 1. Obergeschosses, darüber ist das Haus strahlend weiß verputzt. Die oberen Apartments verfügen über eine windgeschützte Dachterrasse. Die Wohnung vorn an der Ecke kulminiert in einem Bel-

ate flexible ground plans—as unspecific as possible—that could be adapted to changing demands.

In order to counteract the raw winds that pummel the shore of the Öresund almost constantly, the master plan included tall buildings to provide shelter from the wind on the waterfront and a rather labyrinthine housing development with many sheltered corners behind them. Wingårdh used the possibility to combine different types of apartment and widths of building, and so create a structural volume with a remarkably varied and therefore unmistakeable face. In addition, there are diverse window formats—some crosswise and others as high as the room, and sometimes as two-storey glazing overlapping floors, which offers a marvellous view of the Sund and the Öresund Bridge. The main elevation resembles a geometric matrix; it is only possible to distinguish the different floors with effort. The cladding of the lower façade area with natural stone panels provides no helpful indication: it extends over half of the first floor, while above it the house is rendered gleaming white.

vedere, das auch an einen Leuchtturm erinnert und eine traumhafte Rundumsicht bietet. Die Wohnungen sind in der Regel zweigeschossig, wobei die untere Etage mit einem Kalksteinboden und die obere mit Ahornparkett ausgestattet ist. Glas, Edelstahl und Eichenholz bestimmen den Charakter des hochwertigen Innenausbaus.

Der Seitenflügel der Anlage ist niedriger und beherbergt ein Café mit Vorplatz und drei Apartmentgeschosse. Dessen tief gestaffelte Fassade mit schrägen Fensternischen lenkt den Lichteinfall und die Blicke durch keilartige Wandelemente.

Im windgeschützten Bereich hinter dem Vorderhaus steht ein quadratischer Flachbau mit einem kreisrunden Innenhof, Abstellflächen für die Bewohner und Lichthof zur Tiefgarage. Abgeschlossen wird das Ensemble durch einen zweigeschossigen, schmalen Bau, dessen Längsachse zwei langgestreckte, zweigeschossige Wohnungen teilt.

The upper apartments have a roof terrace sheltered from the wind. The apartment at the front corner culminates in a belvedere, which is also reminiscent of a lighthouse and offers a fantastic all-round view. As a rule, the apartments have two floors, whereby the lower storeys have limestone floors and the upper storeys are fitted with maple-wood parquet. Glass, stainless steel, and oak define the character of the high-quality interior design.

The side wing of the complex is lower and accommodates a café with a forecourt and three storeys of apartments. Its steeply graduated façade with sloping window niches directs the fall of light and accentuates the views between wedge-like wall elements.

In the wind-sheltered area behind the front building there is a square-shaped, low structure with a circular inner courtyard, storage space for the residents, and an atrium leading to the underground car park. The ensemble is completed by a slim two-storey building—its axis dividing two long narrow two-storey apartments.

Auditorium und Studentenwerk der Technischen Universität Chalmers, Göteborg (SE)
Auditorium and Student Union Building of Chalmers Technical University, Göteborg (SE)

Es ist schon eine besondere Herausforderung für einen Architekten, wenn er von der Hochschule, an der er studiert hat und an der er selbst lehrt, die Gelegenheit bekommt, just neben den Gebäuden, die seine verehrten Lehrer errichtet haben, mit einem Neubau seine eigene Position darzustellen. Die Aufgabe des eingeladenen Wettbewerbs war Wingårdh auf den Leib geschneidert, ging es doch um ein Haus der Kommunikation, um das Auditorium mit 450 Plätzen und das Studentenwerk der Hochschule mit Café, Pub, Lesezimmer, Musikkeller, Sporthalle und studentischer Selbstverwaltung.

Das neue Studentenzentrum sollte das Gesicht der Universität am Schnittpunkt zwischen Innenstadt und Hochschulgelände prägen. Drei Bestandsbauten waren in das Bauvorhaben zu integrieren, das „die Kirche" genannte alte Studentenwerk, das Melchior Wernstedt 1952 errichtet hatte, die Cafeteria von Lund & Valentin aus dem Jahr 1976 sowie der Hörsaal von Wingårdhs Lehrer Jan Wallinder von 1963. Um das harmonische Zusammengehen auch optisch zu unterstützen, sind Teile des neuen Gebäudes wie der Wernstedt-Bau mit Ziegeln verkleidet, andere mit Schieferplatten wie der Bauteil von Wallinder. Diese Vielfalt verhindert es, dass man das Gebäude als Einheit begreift, sie ist aber auch das Ergebnis der Zurückhaltung des Architekten, der der Versuchung widerstanden hat, die Anlage mit einem großen Wurf zu überformen und sie als sein signifikantes Werk zu präsentieren.

It constitutes a special challenge for any architect when the university at which he once studied and currently teaches gives him an opportunity to present his architectural position with a new building directly beside those constructed by his much-revered teachers. The assignment of the competition among invited participants seemed made to measure for Wingårdh, since it concerned a centre of communication: an auditorium with 450 seats and the university's student union building, including café, pub, reading rooms, music cellar, sports hall, and the students' self-administration office.

The intention of the new student centre was to sharpen the university's profile at the intersection between the inner city and the university campus. Three existing buildings had to be integrated into the construction project: the old student union building known as "the church", which had been built by Melchior Wernstedt in 1952, the cafeteria by Lund & Valentin dating from 1976, and a lecture hall designed by Wingårdh's teacher Jan Wallinder in 1963. In order to underline the favourable structural amalgamation optically, parts of the new building are clad in brick like the Wernstedt building, and others in slate panels like Wallinder's block. This diversity prevents an understanding of the building as a single unit, but it also stems from the architect's own constraint: he withstood the temptation to over-form the complex with a magnificent new design, so presenting it as his most significant work.

Zwei Hauptbaukörper liegen parallel nebeneinander. Der breitere, westliche hat seine Front zum Vorplatz hin und beinhaltet das dreigeschossige Foyer und den Saal, der andere entwickelt sich hinter dem Wallinder-Bau und hat seine Fassade zum Hof hin. Er beherbergt das Studentenwerk.

Mit einem monumentalen Schaufenster wendet sich der Saalbau an seiner Stirnseite der Stadt zu, ein gläsernes Tor gebildet aus kraftvollen Betonstützen und über 18 Meter spannenden Trägern. Der Haupteingang für öffentliche Veranstaltungen mit dem Foyer und darüber die zweigeschossige Lobby des großen Saals haben Ausblick auf den Vorplatz und leuchten am Abend einladend in die Stadt. Helles Birkenholz an der Außenwand des Auditoriums bestimmt den freundlichen Charakter der Lobby, helles Birkenholz beeinflusst auch die Stimmung im Inneren des Saals.

Das Foyer am Haupteingang ist zudem Auftakt zu einem abwechslungsreichen Raumkontinuum, das sich diagonal durch die Gebäude bis in den rückwärtigen Bereich zur Cafeteria zieht und mit seinen Erschließungswegen das Ensemble auch in der Vertikalen bis in die Höhe des zweiten Obergeschosses durchdringt. Dabei öffnet und verbindet es kommunikative Raumsequenzen wie das Café und den Pub und erlaubt Einblicke in die angelagerten Nutzungen, dient der Orientierung und ist belebte Verkehrsfläche und Aufenthaltsbereich zugleich. Mit dieser zwischen die Gebäude geschobenen und durch Oberlichter erhellten Erschließungszone, in der sich die

The two main volumes of the building are set parallel to each other; the wide western part faces onto the forecourt and accommodates the three-storey foyer and the hall, the other extends behind the Wallinder-building with its façade facing the courtyard. It houses the student union.

A monumental window at the end of the hall building faces towards the city—a glazed portal comprising solid concrete supports and girders spanning more than eighteen metres. The main entrance for public events, the foyer, and the two-storey lobby of the great hall above it offer a view towards the forecourt and shine out into the city invitingly after dark. Light-coloured birch wood on the outer wall of the auditorium defines the friendly character of the lobby, and birch wood also helps create the atmosphere in the hall's interior.

The foyer by the main entrance represents the start of a sequence of diverse rooms running diagonally through the building to the cafeteria at the back. It also provides vertical access to the ensemble up to the height of the second floor, thereby opening up and connecting communicative sequences of rooms like the café and the pub, and providing views of adjacent functions. Both lively circulation area and recreational space, it also serves general orientation. This access zone inserted between the buildings, illuminated by skylights, combines impressions of inside and out and helps the architect to link—on different levels—the older small-scale student

Eindrücke von innen und außen vermischen, ist es gelungen, den kleinmaßstäblichen alten Studentenklub sowie die Cafeteria auf verschiedenen Ebenen mit dem großformatigeren Neubau räumlich und funktional zu verknüpfen.

An der Seitenfront orientiert sich das Ensemble mit seiner zweiten Eingangssituation zum studentischen Campus hin. Ein gläsernes Café mit dem Angebot, drinnen und draußen zu sitzen, lädt zum Plausch ein. Im Obergeschoss hängt ein erstaunlich weit vorkragender Balkon vor dem kleinen Auditorium als Austritt für Raucher in der Veranstaltungspause oder als theatralische Redebühne bei Versammlungen im Hof.

Durch die klare, disziplinierte, letztlich etwas zurückhaltendere Formensprache ist die Verbindung zu den drei Altbauteilen hergestellt und hält sich die optische Komplexität der räumlichen Vielfalt in angenehmen Grenzen. Die durch das formale Zusammenspiel mit der Umgebung motivierte formale Strenge und Ordnung der Fassaden steht in gewissem Gegensatz zu den frei fließenden inneren Räumen, in denen das kommunikative Element als Organisations- und Gestaltungsprämisse im Vordergrund steht.

Die Anlage hat sich inzwischen wie erwartet zum attraktiven Zentrum mit vielfältigen Bezügen zum Campus entwickelt, zum lebendigen Ort mit studentischen Aktivitäten bis in den späten Abend. Gert Wingårdh hat dafür 2001 seinen dritten Kasper Salin Preis erhalten.

club and the cafeteria to the bigger-scale new building, in both spatial and functional terms.

The second entrance at the side gives the ensemble an orientation towards the student campus. A glazed café with seating both inside and outside extends an invitation to linger and chat. Its balcony on the upper floor projects to a surprising extent, hanging in front of the small auditorium as a place for smokers to step out during breaks or as a dramatic podium for speakers when meetings are held in the courtyard.

The ensemble's clear, disciplined, ultimately rather constrained formal language helps to generate a link to the three old parts of the building, while the visual complexity of the diverse architecture on site is thus limited and remains attractive. The formal severity and order of the façades—which is motivated by interplay with the surroundings—contrasts to some extent with the freely flowing interior spaces, in which the communicative element is accentuated as a result of organisational and design premises.

As anticipated, the complex has developed into an attractive centre with diverse references to the campus—a lively setting for student activities until well into the night. Gert Wingårdh received his third Kasper Salin Prize for the design in 2001.

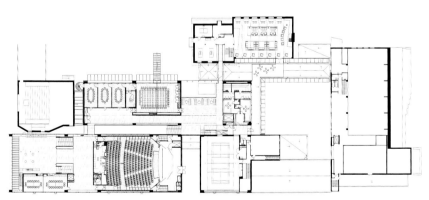

Piano Pavillon, Lahti (FI)
Piano Pavilion, Lahti (FI)

Der Pavillon im 100 Kilometer nördlich von Helsinki gelegenen Lahti ist eine Reminiszenz an den Architekten Renzo Piano, der im Jahr 2000 mit dem Preis für Holzarchitektur „Spirit of Nature" der finnischen Holzindustrie ausgezeichnet wurde und als Teil des Preises den Auftrag für ein Café im Hafen von Lahti bekommen sollte. Doch Piano war zu beschäftigt und konnte den Auftrag nicht annehmen; so baute Gert Wingårdh das Objekt unmittelbar vor der Sibeliushalle Piano zu Ehren. Wingårdh, der sich stilistisch nicht festlegen lässt, fiel es leicht, das Gebäude im Sinne Renzo Pianos zu entwerfen. Aus Holz natürlich, denn als Investor trat eine Holzbaufirma auf den Plan und der Pavillon ist Teil des Holzarchitekturparks, der im Quartier am Ufer des Vesijärvisees im Entstehen ist. Ein kleines Café sollte es sein, rundum verglast, um die Aussicht zu nutzen; dazu Küche, Theke und Nebenräume, alles recht knapp bemessen, sowie die umlaufende Terrasse für den Sommerbetrieb.

Auf eine über die Uferlinie auskragende, von Stahlträgern getragene Grundplatte stellte der Architekt ein eingeschossiges Rahmentragwerk aus 50 Zentimeter starken Leimholzbindern, in das die flach parabolisch gebogenen Sparren des Daches „eingehängt" sind. Die sehr schmalen, hochrechteckigen Pfetten unter dem Glasdach bestehen aus Kerto-Furnierschichtholz aus finnischer Fichte. Auch bei den Wänden kam Kerto zum Einsatz, der Innenboden besteht aus Parkett. Die Decken im Terrassenbereich aus Birkensperrholz sind perforiert und lassen gefiltertes Licht in das Café einfallen. Die bewitterte Terrasse ist mit Dielen aus einem wetterfesten Holz-Kunststoff-Kompositmaterial belegt. Aus Espenholz gedrehte Rundhölzer ragen wie eine Reihe von Augenwimpern an der Seeseite über das Dach hinaus und bilden einen Sonnenschutzschirm. Je nach Blickwinkel assoziieren sie Rahen, Fischgräten oder Angelruten.

Durch die Geländer aus rahmenlosem Sicherheitsglas wirkt die Grundplatte ebenso schlank wie das auf den soliden Rahmen auflastende, fast filigrane Dachtragwerk, das mit der aufgelegten Glasscheibe kaum etwas zu tragen haben scheint. Das kleine Café ist perfekt situiert und bildet einen angenehmen Rahmen für den Aussichtspunkt, von dem aus man den Blick weit über den See schweifen lassen kann.

The pavilion in Lahti—one hundred kilometres north of Helsinki—is intended to remind us of the architect Renzo Piano, who received the "Spirit of Nature" award for wooden architecture from the Finnish timber industry in 2000. Part of the award was a contract to build a café in the harbour area of Lahti. However, Piano was too busy to accept this commission and so Gert Wingårdh built the café directly in front of the Sibelius Hall in honour of Piano. Since it is difficult to pin down Wingårdh's style anyway, he had no trouble designing the building entirely in the spirit of Renzo Piano. It is made of wood, naturally, since the participating investor was a timber construction company and the pavilion was to be part of the wooden architecture park that is being developed in the district on the shore of Vesijärvi Lake. It was to be a small café, fully glazed to exploit the view, and incorporating kitchen, counter, and auxiliary rooms all on a very small scale—as well as a terrace for summer business around its full circumference.

On a foundation slab resting on steel supports and projecting over the shoreline, the architect placed a single-storey, frame load-bearing structure made from fifty-centimetre-thick laminated timber trusses, into which the flat, parabolic rafters of the roof are "hung". The very narrow, upright rectangular purlins below the glass roof consist of "Kerto" laminated timbers made from Finnish fir. Kerto was also employed on the walls, and the floor inside is parquet. The birch plywood ceiling decks in the terrace area are perforated, allowing filtered light to fall into the café. The weathered terrace comprises boards made of a weather-fast wood and plastic composite material. Round timbers turned in aspen wood project from the roof like a series of eyelashes on the lake side, creating a protective sunshade. Depending on one's perspective, they trigger associations with nautical yards, fish bones, or fishing rods.

Through the railings of frameless safety glass, the foundation slab appears as slender as the almost filigree roof-bearing structure on the solid frame, which seems to have very little to carry with the glass pane on top. The small café is perfectly situated and provides a pleasant setting for the vantage point, from which one can survey much of the lake.

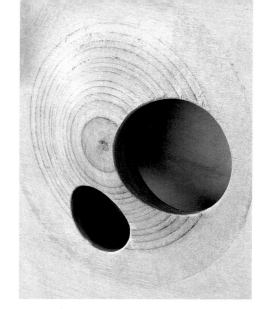

DETAIL: **TÜRGRIFF** DETAIL: DOOR HANDLE

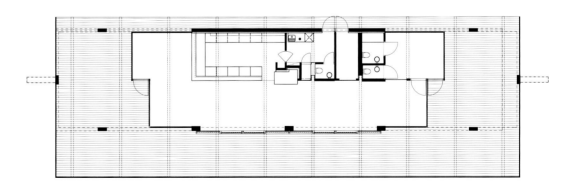

Zitadellenbad, Landskrona (SE)
Swimming Pool "Zitadellenbad", Landskrona (SE)

Die Wasserwelt ist nicht nur Inhalt, sondern auch Motiv für die Gestaltung der Erweiterung des Freibads von Landskrona. Auf einer Landzunge zwischen Öresund, Zitadelle und Hafen lag das alte Bad aus dem Jahr 1967 mit einem kleinen Becken, einem 50-Meter-Meerwasserbecken und einer kleinen Tribüne. Die neuen, eingeschossigen Funktionsbauten des Bades bilden einen gegen die Küstenwinde schützenden Winkel. Sie bieten Raum für die Umkleidekabinen und ein Café, aus dem heraus die Kleinkinder im Planschbecken beaufsichtigt werden können. Der kürzere Schenkel des Winkels beinhaltet Betriebsräume und Büros.

Ein Sprungbecken mit Sprungturm und ein Kinderplanschbecken kamen hinzu. Der sich nach oben konisch erweiternde Kampfrichterturm mit Aussichtsterrasse ist ein Echo des hinter der Anlage stehenden signifikanten Wasserturms.

Azurblau und Türkis, die Farben des Mittelmeers, und die blauen Schatten unter der südlichen Sonne scheinen beim winkelförmigen Gebäude auf. Es hat in zwei Blautönungen gefärbte, geschosshohe Glaspaneele als Fassaden. Außerdem rinnt ein stetiger Wasserfilm die Wände hinab und bringt sie zum Glitzern wie die sonnenbeschienene See: ein vertikaler Pool neben den drei horizontalen. Im laufenden Wasser spiegeln sich Himmel und Wasserreflexe der Pools. Aber auch das Meer ist präsent, denn durch Lücken im Umkleidetrakt ist aus sicherer Warte der Öresund zu sehen.

David Hockneys farbenfrohe Bilder von Schwimmbecken gaben die Anregung für die Glasmosaikbilder von Wasserringen auf dem Boden inner- und außerhalb der Umkleidekabinen. So leuchten nicht nur die Wasserbecken in sattem Azurblau, sondern das gesamte Ensemble wird zum kühlenden, erfrischenden Sommererlebnis.

The world of water is not only the content, but also the motif employed in the design of this extension to an open-air pool in Landskrona. The old baths dating from 1967 had a small pool, a fifty-metre salt-water pool and a small grandstand, and were situated on a peninsular between the Öresund, the citadel and the harbour. The new, single-storey functional buildings of the baths meet at an angle, providing shelter from the coastal winds. They offer space for changing rooms and a café, from which it is possible to supervise small children in the paddling pool area. The shorter wing contains operating areas and offices.

A diving pool with diving tower and a children's paddling area have also been added. The competition judges' tower with its viewing terrace is shaped like a cone widening towards the top, echoing the striking water tower behind the pool complex.

Azure blue and turquoise, the colours of the Mediterranean, and the blue shadows under a southern sun appear in the angle-shaped building. The façades consist of storey-high glass panels in two different shades of blue. A continual film of water runs down the walls and makes them glitter like the sunshine on the sea: a vertical pool beside the three horizontal ones. The sky and the highlights on the pool water are reflected in this running moisture. But the sea is also present, as gaps in the changing wing offer glimpses of the Öresund from the safety of the baths.

David Hockney's colourful images of swimming pools provided the inspiration for the glass mosaic pictures of swim-rings on the floor inside and outside the changing rooms. Now it is not only the pools that glitter in a deep azure blue; the whole ensemble has been developed into a cooling, refreshing summer experience.

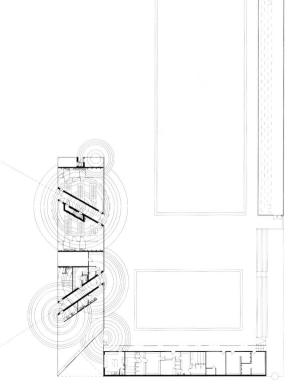

Kontrollturm Arlanda International Airport, Sigtuna (SE)
Control Tower at Arlanda International Airport, Sigtuna (SE)

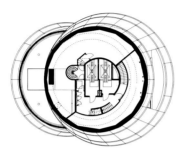 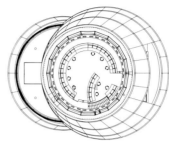

Der Ausbau des Stockholmer Flughafens Arlanda International mit neuen Rollbahnen und Terminals für bis zu 25 Millionen Fluggäste pro Jahr machte auch den Neubau eines Kontrollturms notwendig. Die Beobachtungs- und Radartürme der Flugüberwachung sind meist die primär wahrgenommenen Baulichkeiten der Flughäfen, und oft ist der Kontrollturm jenes Gebäude, dessen Bild am besten im Gedächtnis der Reisenden haften bleibt.

Gert Wingårdh nahm die Gelegenheit wahr, ein *signature building* zu entwerfen, ein Wahrzeichen, das für die Fluggäste einen hohen Wiedererkennungswert besitzt und für den Airport Arlanda steht. Die Silhouette ist mit zwei Vögeln verglichen worden, zwei Kranichen vielleicht, die ihre Köpfe zusammenstecken. Der 80 Meter hohe Turmschaft besteht tatsächlich aus zwei „Hälsen", zwei im Grundriss sich überlappende Kreise, fünf Meter im Durchmesser der eine, neun Meter der andere. Der Sockelbau bleibt dabei im Bild, denn er gleicht zwei ausgebreiteten Flügeln.

Dem Gliederungsprinzip der klassischen Säule mit Basis, Schaft und Kapitell entsprechend zeigt der Turm Sockel, Schaft und Kopf. Den beiden gekuppelten Schäften entsprechen die sich gleichfalls überschneidenden, dynamisch geformten Turmkanzeln, die den Fluglotsen den notwendigen Überblick verschaffen. Die obere Kanzel dient der Überwachung der Flüge, Starts und Landungen, die untere der Steuerung des Bodenverkehrs auf den Taxiways und auf dem Vor-

The expansion of Stockholm's Arlanda International Airport to provide new runways and terminals for up to twenty-five million passengers annually also made it necessary to erect a new control tower. Generally speaking, flight surveillance and radio towers are the airport structures which are perceived first, and the control tower in particular will often remain in the traveller's memory.

Gert Wingårdh grasped this opportunity to design a signature building: a landmark easily recognised by flight passengers, which would become representative of Arlanda Airport. The silhouette has been compared to two birds, perhaps two cranes with their heads close together. Indeed, the eighty-metre-high shaft of the tower does consist of two "necks": two circular towers with overlapping diameters of five and nine metres respectively. The base building persists with the image, as it resembles two outstretched wings.

In accordance with the principle of the classical column—which is divided into base, shaft and capital—the tower may also be perceived as base, shaft, and head. The two merging shafts also correspond to the intersecting, dynamically formed chancels, which provide the air-traffic controllers with the essential all-round view. The upper chancel is for the supervision of flights, take-offs, and landings; the other is for control over ground traffic on the taxiways and apron. The base building houses operational and auxiliary rooms, offices, a canteen, and a small lecture room.

feld. Im Sockelgebäude sind die Betriebs- und Nebenräume, Büros, Kantine und ein kleiner Hörsaal untergebracht.

In der Grundfarbe, der eine weiß, der andere schwarz, erinnern die Türme mit ihrem Streifendekor an Leuchttürme für die Seefahrt. Wingårdhs Vorliebe für die Kunst des 20. Jahrhunderts, in diesem Fall die Op-Art der sechziger Jahre, kommt bei der Farbgebung zum Tragen. Doch auch die Gegenwartskunst kommt zum Zug, denn die Künstlerin Silja Ratanen hat die Streifen der Schäfte mit Zitaten aus Antoine de Saint-Exupérys Roman *Südkurier* beschriftet.

Mit dem Thema der Vögel und der typografischen Kunst sowie den dynamistischen Formen als narrative Attribute wird das technische Funktionsgebäude mit einem offenkundigen Symbolismus aufgeladen, der den Bau gegenüber den eher pragmatischen Betriebsgebäuden zu seinen Füßen adelt und als besonders bedeutend kennzeichnet.

The towers' basic colours—one white and the other black—create a striped décor reminiscent of lighthouses for shipping. Gert Wingårdh's choice of colours was influenced by his liking for twentieth century art, in this case the Op-Art of the sixties. But contemporary art also gets a look-in: artist Silja Ratanen had quotations from Antoine de Saint-Exupéry's novel *Southern Mail* written on the stripes of the shafts.

The bird theme, the typographical art, and its own dynamic forms as a narrative attribute charge the technical-functional building with obvious symbolism; by contrast to the rather pragmatic buildings below, this gives the structure dignity—picking it out as especially important.

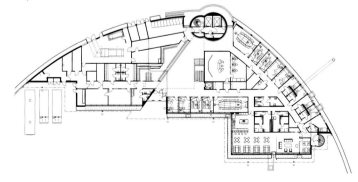

K:fem Warenhaus, Vällingby (SE)
K:fem Department Store, Vällingby (SE)

Die 1954 eröffnete Trabantenstadt Vällingby, nördlich von Stockholm gelegen, war in die Jahre gekommen. Die Einwohnerschaft war überaltert, die Geschäfte verödeten. Nach 50 Jahren begann nun die Renaissance mit dem neuen Stadteingang und dem erneuerten urbanen Zentrum mit der glasgedeckten Einkaufsmeile über dem U-Bahnhof. Deren südliches Ende bildet das K:fem Warenhaus, ein Einkaufstempel von betörendem Glanz, der wie ein kostbares Juwel am Kopf des Zentrums steht und es erheblich aufwertet. Ein beängstigend weit auskragendes, signalrot gefärbtes Dach ragt über die Ecke und ist bereits von Weitem als Wahrzeichen zu sehen. Wie es sich für einen Konsumtempel gehört, sind die Logos der Modelabel an den roten Himmel geschrieben und leuchten von innen lockend und verheißungsvoll.

Die mit einer Haut aus Glasscheiben überzogene Fassade wirkt mal transluzent, mal transparent und hat eine unergründliche Tiefe. Die aufgedruckten weißen Punkte verflüchtigen sich in der Höhe, der dünne, weiße Schleier wird nach oben hin immer durchsichtiger und lässt die dahinter liegende rote Metallwand durchscheinen. Nachts wird die Fassade hinterleuchtet und bringt den Bau blutrot zum Glühen. Wo sich früher das überdimensionale „V" als Wahrzeichen Vällingbys und als Victory-Zeichen für den Wohlfahrtsstaat drehte, strahlt heute das K:fem als neue Ikone der Konsumgesellschaft.

An der Südecke ist der ansonsten klare, ungestörte Baukörper aufgeschnitten, gibt auf breiter Front den Eingang frei und saugt die potenziellen Kunden geradezu in sein Inneres. Drinnen empfängt den Käufer eine hell erleuchtete weiße Sphäre, auch sie mit halbtransparenten, schemenhaften Raumgrenzen, mit einer weißen Wendeltreppe und Fahrtreppen, die wie Skulpturen im zentralen Lichthof stehen. Man fühlt sich an die entmaterialisierte Architektur der japanischen Architekten SANAA erinnert, bei der Weiß als Abwesenheit von Farbe definiert ist.

Im Hintergrund führt eine schmale Passage in den kleinen dreieckigen Anbau einer exklusiven Boutique, der durch die Fußgängerzone vom Hauptgebäude getrennt ist und der im Kontrast zur weißen Welt des K:fem mit tiefschwarzem Glas bekleidet ist.

Der K:fem Multi Fashion Store nobler Marken lockt auch modebewusste Stockholmer zum standesgemäßen Shoppen in den Vorort.

Founded in 1954, the satellite town Vällingby, north of Stockholm, had been beginning to feel its age. The population was aging rapidly, and the shops were becoming somewhat desolate. After fifty years, a renaissance began with a new entry into the town, and the town centre's renewal in the shape of a glass-roofed shopping mile above the underground station. At the south end one can find K:fem department store—a shopping temple of dizzying splendour situated at the head of the centre like a precious gem, greatly adding to its merit. The bright-red roof with its disturbing overhang projects above the corner, already visible from some distance: a new landmark. As fitting for any consumer temple, the logos of fashion labels are written onto this red sky, glowing from within, tempting, and full of promise.

The facade is covered in a membrane of glass panels; sometimes this appears translucent and at other times transparent, suggesting an unfathomable depth. The white dots printed on the membrane evaporate towards the top: the thin white veil becomes more and more transparent as it approaches the roof, permitting us to see through to the red metal wall behind. At night the façade is back-lit, making the building glow in a blood-red colour. Where an oversized "V" once revolved as a landmark of Vällingby and a victory-sign for the welfare state, the gleaming K:fem is radiant today—a new icon of the consumer society.

At the south corner the otherwise, uninterrupted building is cut open, revealing the entrance within a wide frontage and drawing potential customers inside almost physically. Here, the buyer is greeted by a brightly-lit white sphere with semi-transparent, only vaguely sketched contours; a white spiral staircase and elevators are positioned in the central atrium like sculptures. One is reminded of the Japanese architects SANAA and their dematerialised architecture, whereby white is defined as an absence of colour.

At the back, a narrow passage leads into another small, triangular-shaped building that houses an exclusive boutique, separated from the main building by the pedestrian zone, and clad—in contrast to the white world of K:fem—in deep black glass.

K:fem department store for exclusive brands attracts fashion-conscious Stockholmers to the suburb to shop in style.

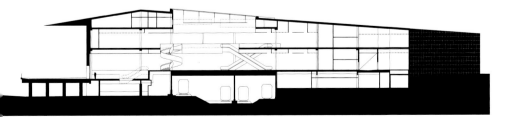

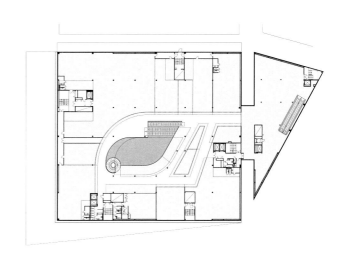

Universeum, Göteborg (SE)

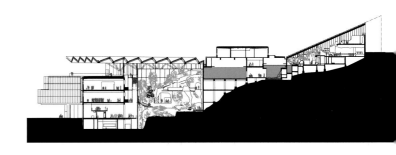

Wie packt man einen steilen Berg in ein Gebäude? Und wie bringt man vier unterschiedliche Nutzungen zusammen? Vor diesen Fragen stand Gert Wingårdh beim Entwurf des Wissenschaftszentrums. Der Regionalverband Göteborg, die Technische Universität Chalmers, die Universität Göteborg sowie die westschwedische Industrie- und Handelskammer hatten sich zusammengetan, um ein Museum zu errichten, das jungen Menschen Naturwissenschaften und Technik näherbringen soll. Als Bauplatz wählten sie ein steiles Grundstück am Ostrand der Stadterweiterung aus dem 19. Jahrhundert nahe dem Kongresszentrum und unmittelbar neben dem Liseberg-Vergnügungspark. Die Hauptfassade des Universeums wendet sich dem belebten Verkehrsknoten Korsvägen zu. In dessen Mitte steht ein kleiner dreieckiger Kiosk, den ebenfalls Wingårdh entworfen hatte und der mit seiner Form schon auf den Neubau hinzuweisen scheint.

Mit einer dramatisch vorschießenden Ecke und einer Eingangssituation von magnetischer Anziehungskraft drängt das Universeum in den Platzraum. Die links anschließende, in den Berg laufende haushohe Glasfassade verdoppelt sich spiegelnd im Wasserbecken vor dem Felsen, lässt ihr Inneres durchscheinen und weckt Neugier. Über allem schwebt ein filigranes, sägezahnartiges Dachtragwerk aus Fachwerk-Leimbindern von beeindruckender Auskragung.

How do you pack a steep hill inside a building? And how do you combine four different types of use? Gert Wingårdh faced these questions when designing the science centre. Göteborg Region Association of Local Authorities, Chalmers University of Technology, Göteborg University, and the West Sweden Chamber of Commerce and Industry had come together to construct a museum which aimed to familiarise young people with the natural sciences and technology. They selected a steep plot on the edge of the nineteenth century city expansion area—close to the congress centre, and directly alongside Liseberg Pleasure Park—as the construction site. The main façade of the Universeum faces onto the busy traffic junction Korsvägen. At the centre of this junction there is a small triangular kiosk that Wingårdh had also designed earlier: its form already seems to point to the new building.

The Universeum penetrates into the space of the junction with a dramatically advancing corner and a magnetically attractive entrance area. Directly to the left of the entrance, a glass façade as high as a house runs into the hillside, reflected and doubled in the water pool in front of the rock. The interior shines through to the outside, arousing the curiosity of passers-by. Floating above all this, with an extremely impressive overhang, is the filigree saw-tooth roof bearing structure made of glue-laminated timbers.

Der Eingangsbau entlang dem auf Korsvägen zulaufenden Söda Vägen ist das Wissenschaftsmuseum, die Glasfassade gehört zur Einhausung des tropischen Regenwaldes. Östlich schließen sich das als steinerne Box konzipierte Aquarium sowie ein Glashaus an, in dem Biotope schwedischer Landschaften en miniature zu erleben sind. Wingårdh nutzte die unterschiedlichen Anforderungen vom voll besonnten Wintergarten bis zum total introvertierten, mit Kunstlicht ausgestatteten Aquarium, um eine spannungsreiche Collage zusammenzufügen und dem Gebäude ein signifikantes Gesicht zu geben.

Das Ausstellungsgebäude – das „hölzerne Langhaus" – ist eine kraftvolle Holzkonstruktion, die mit ihren mächtigen Stützen und den offenen Holzbalkendecken auch im Inneren atmosphärisch Wirkung entfaltet. Holzverkleidete Wände und Fußböden vervollständigen den Raumeindruck, der sich von den gestalterisch neutral gehaltenen Schauräumen anderer Wissenschaftsmuseen doch stark unterscheidet.

Der weitgehend geschlossene Baukörper des Aquariums zeigt nach außen eine Gabionenfassade aus Drahtkörben, die mit Bruchstein gefüllt sind, während das anschließende, steil aufragende Glashaus der schwedischen Landschaften als allseits transparentes Prisma die Spitze des Felsens erobert.

Der Rundgang beginnt nach Ticketkauf und Durchquerung der Eingangshalle an der Südseite des Gebäudes, wo zwei außen liegende

The entrance building along the road Söda Vägen leading to Korsvägen is the science museum, the glass façade belonging to the space accommodating the tropical rain forest. In the east, this is abutted by the stone box of the aquarium, and a glasshouse in which it is possible to experience Swedish landscapes *en miniature* in a biotope. Wingårdh employed the different demands—ranging from a winter garden requiring full sunshine to the completely introverted aquarium, equipped with artificial light—in order to create an exciting collage and give the building a striking appearance.

The exhibition building—the "wooden longhouse"—is a visibly weighty wooden construction generating, in the interior too, an atmospheric effect with its massive supports and the open wooden beams of the ceiling. Wood-clad walls and floors complete the impression, which differs greatly from the display rooms of other science museums, whose design is generally kept neutral.

The predominantly closed structural volume of the aquarium has a façade of gabions (wire baskets) on the outside. These are filled with rubble, while the adjacent, steeply rising glasshouse of Swedish landscapes occupies the top of the hill as a transparent prism visible from all around.

The round tour begins after buying a ticket and crossing the entrance hall on the south side of the building, where two external, oblique lifts take visitors twenty-six metres higher up to the top of the hill. First, the circuit leads into the glazed prism, passing

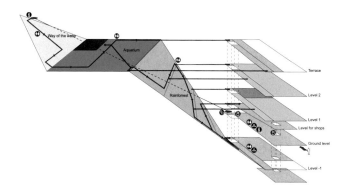

Schrägaufzüge die Besucher 26 Meter höher auf die Höhe des Felsens bringen. Zunächst führt der Weg im gläsernen Prisma durch schwedische Lande von den arktischen Wäldern bis zu den Inseln im Südosten und zur Ostseeküste Skågenes, dann durch das dunkle Aquarium mit der effektvoll illuminierten Tierwelt von Nordsee und Atlantik. Sodann, wieder im Tageslicht, geht es im Tropenhaus über Serpentinenpfade den steilen Felsen hinab durch den tropischen Regenwald. Nebenbei gibt es auf verschiedenen Ebenen Verbindungsbrücken zum großen Treppenhaus und von dort auf die große Dachterrasse und in die beiden Ebenen des Ausstellungsgebäudes, wo Dauer- und Wechselausstellungen Technikgeschichte und Naturwissenschaften thematisieren. Auf dem Weg zum Veranstaltungssaal im Untergeschoss sind am Grund des Regenwalds noch die Riesenschlangen und die tropischen Fische zu bewundern.

Wie immer legte Wingårdh großen Wert auf die ökologischen Kenndaten des Gebäudes. Das Gebäude ist energietechnisch auf geringen Verbrauch hin optimiert. Fortgeschrittene Systeme für Wasser- und Abfallrecycling sind eingebaut. Die Sägezahnform des Daches ist für die Aufnahme von Photovoltaikpaneelen konzipiert, wozu es jedoch nur zu Teilen gekommen ist. Die weitgehende Verwendung des nachwachsenden Baustoffs Holz trägt zur Nachhaltigkeit des Bauwerks bei.

Das Universeum ist eine der Naturvermittlung gewidmete Institution. Gert Wingårdh versteht deshalb auch das Gebäude selbst als ein didaktisches Projekt des Museums und hat es in diesem Sinn gestaltet und konstruiert.

through Swedish countryside from the Arctic forests to the islands in the south-east and the Baltic coast of Skågen, and then enters the dark aquarium with its effectively illuminated North Sea and Atlantic fauna. Back in the daylight, serpentine paths lead down the steep cliff through the tropical rain forest within the glasshouse. On various levels in between, there are linking piers to the main stairwell, and from there onto the extensive roof terrace and the two levels of the exhibition building, where permanent and changing exhibitions examine the history of technology and the natural sciences. On the way to the events hall on the basement floor, it is possible to admire giant snakes and tropical fish on the bed of the rain forest.

As always, Wingårdh paid particular attention to the building's ecological features. Its energy technology is optimised for low consumption. Advanced systems for recycling water and refuse are installed. The saw-tooth form of the roof is designed for the mounting of photovoltaic panels—although this has only been partially implemented. The comprehensive use of wood as a renewable building material contributes to the sustainability of the construction.

The Universeum is an institution dedicated to the understanding and presentation of nature. As a consequence, Gert Wingårdh views the building itself as one of the museum's didactic projects, and has designed and constructed it in this spirit.

Sign Hotel, Stockholm (SE)

Das Grundstück des Hotels liegt zentral, nur ein paar Schritte vom Hauptbahnhof entfernt und hat eine lange, repräsentative Front nach Südwesten. Diese Front ließ sich jedoch wegen der Störungen durch den Verschiebebahnhof vor dem Haus nicht für Gästezimmer nutzen. So legte Wingårdh die Erschließungsflure an diese Seite und machte die Fassade zum unverkennbaren Stadtzeichen. Mit schwarzem chinesischem Granit verkleidet, der in horizontalen Streifen mal poliert tiefschwarz, mal gestockt hellgrau, mal grob gebrochen dunkelgrau erscheint, malte er das Motiv der benachbarten Schienenstränge in abstrahierter Form an die Fassade. Das Hotel wird zum weithin sichtbaren Stadtzeichen und prägt das ganze Bahnhofsviertel.

Die beiden Flügel des Hauses laufen nach Süden aufeinander zu und lassen zwischen ihren messerscharfen Spitzen zum Hauptbahnhof hin eine kleine Schaufront frei, die in ihrer dramatischen Dynamik ebenfalls zeichenhaft, unverwechselbar und markenbildend wirkt.

Die Eingangsfront an der Ostseite öffnet sich mit ihrer zweigeschossigen Halle als Verlängerung des öffentlichen Raumes des Norra Bantorget Platzes. Die Hauptfassade neigt sich leicht gegen den Platz und spiegelt mit ihren Granit- und Glasflächen das Grün des Parks wider. Sie ist durch haushohe, eingetiefte Pfeiler in fünf einzelne „Häuser" unterteilt und bildet so eine die Stadtstruktur berücksichtigende, gegliederte Fassadenabwicklung.

Beim Design der Innenarchitektur des Hotels ist die klare, schnörkellose Sprache weitergeführt. Die Gäste aus anderen Ländern erkennen bei der Möblierung die Klassiker der skandinavischen Gestaltungskultur wieder, die sie in ihren Designmuseen gesehen haben. Auch durch die Wandbilder sind die vier skandinavischen Länder in den Zimmern präsent.

The hotel site is central, only a few yards away from the main station. It has a long, representative front facing south-west, but this could not be utilised for guest rooms because of disturbance from the shunting yard alongside the plot. Wingårdh therefore placed the corridors on this side and turned the façade into an unmistakeable urban landmark. Cladding it in black Chinese granite that shows up as horizontal stripes—some polished to a deep black, others a granulated light grey, and others a rough-broken dark grey—, Wingårdh "painted" the façade with the motif of the neighbouring tracks in an abstract form. The hotel is turned into a symbol visible from far away, one that shapes the whole of the station district.

The two wings of the building are angled towards each other in a southerly direction; their sharp ends point towards the main station, leaving only a small front open to view. Here, the dramatic dynamics of the architecture also appear symbolic; a new, unmistakeable city landmark is created.

With its two-storey entrance hall, the eastern front opens out as if extending the public space of Norra Bantorget Square. The main façade leans slightly towards the square, reflecting the green of the park in its granite and glass surfaces. It is divided into five separate "houses" by inset columns to roof height, thus creating the effect of a divided façade and echoing the surrounding urban structures. This clear, unembellished language is continued in the hotel's interior design. Guests from other countries will recognise the classics of Scandinavian design culture in the furnishings; they have seen them already in design museums. The presence of all four Scandinavian countries is conjured by murals in the rooms.

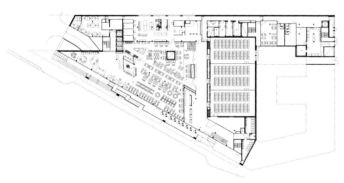

Knotenpunkt Mölndalbrücke, Mölndal (SE)
Junction Mölndal Bridge, Mölndal (SE)

Neben AstraZeneca ist in Mölndal südlich von Göteborg ein weiteres von Gert Wingårdh entworfenes Wahrzeichen anzutreffen. Es handelt sich um einen Verkehrsknotenpunkt für den Bus- und Eisenbahnverkehr. Wo die Mölndalbrücke die Autobahn E6/E20 und die Bahnlinie nach Süden Richtung Malmö überquert, gibt es Umsteigemöglichkeiten zwischen den Vorort- und Fernzügen sowie den Straßenbahn- und Buslinien unter der Brücke und dem Busverkehr auf Brückenniveau. Zu gestalten waren Fahrtreppenverbindungen und Lifte, Schutzdächer für die Fußwege und Wartebereiche, windgeschützte Sitzgelegenheiten, Warteräume und ein Café.

Wingårdh gab jeder Fußwegspur ein schmales Schutzdach, wodurch sich ein lang gestrecktes Netz von einem Ende der Brücke zum anderen und eine leichte Konstruktion ergaben. Durch die eingekerbten Dachkanten mit spitzen Ausläufen an den Dachenden erscheinen die Dächer ebenfalls optisch leichter und dynamischer. Ihre Unterseiten und die Stützen sind mit unbehandeltem Lärchenholz verkleidet.

Aufgänge, Café und Windschutzwände sind vollflächig verglast. Einige der Scheiben sind in warmen gelben und violetten Zwischentönen farbig angelegt, erzeugen Lichteffekte auf Wänden und Fußboden und beeinflussen die Lichtstimmung.

Mit seinen eleganten Formen und ungewöhnlichen Farben ist der Knotenpunkt leicht wiederzuerkennen und somit Signal und Orientierungspunkt für aus- und umsteigende Reisende. Das Café hat direkte Verbindung zum Orts- und Einkaufszentrum von Mölndal.

In addition to AstraZeneca, one encounters another landmark designed by Gert Wingårdh in Mölndal, south of Göteborg: a junction for bus and train traffic. At the point where Mölndal Bridge crosses the motorway E6/E20 and the train line south towards Malmö, it is possible to change trains below the bridge from local to long-distance lines, as well as between several tram lines—and on the level of the bridge, between bus routes. The design had to include moving staircases and lifts, as well as sheltering roofs for the walkways and waiting areas, wind-sheltered places to sit, waiting rooms, and a café.

Wingårdh gave every walkway a narrow roof, creating a sheltering network extending from one end of the bridge to the other, and a light construction. The notched roof edges with sharp terminating outlets also make the roofs appear lighter and more dynamic. Their undersides and structural supports are clad in untreated larch wood.

The stairs, café, and walls protecting from the wind are all fully glazed. Some of the glass panes are toned in shades of warm yellow and violet, creating light effects on the walls and floors and influencing the atmosphere.

The junction's elegant forms and unusual colours make it easy for travellers to recognise, and so it has become a signal and an orientation point for those leaving and changing public transport. There is a direct link to the shopping mall and town centre of Mölndal from the café.

Mit großer Geste empfängt das Bürogebäude mit seinem neunge-schossigen gläsernen Atrium den Besucher. Ein weit auskragendes, zeichenhaftes Vordach adelt das Vorfahren und Aussteigen zur Zere-monie. Im haushohen Foyer kann man die vielen Mitarbeiter erah-nen, die hinter den Galeriebrüstungen tätig sind. Im Foyer beginnt auch die Achse durch das Firmengelände, mit der alle Betriebsge-bäude erschlossen sind.

Als Gert Wingårdh 1989 in das Projekt eintrat, hatte der Pharmaher-steller Hässle (später AstraZeneca) auf dem neuen Firmengelände südlich von Göteborg bereits einige sehr unterschiedliche Bauten errichtet. Die Aufgabe bestand darin, die Anlage durch eine Vielzahl von neuen Labor- und Technikgebäuden stark zu verdichten und die-se mit den Bestandsbauten optisch und betriebstechnisch zu einem funktionierenden Organismus zusammenzuführen.

Die Neubauten sind in einer vom Bestand vorgegebenen orthogo-nalen Ordnung hinzugefügt, vermeiden aber durch den Wechsel von längs- und quergerichteten Baukörpern eine monotone Reihung. Die Baukörper sind in Länge und Breite je nach den funktionalen Erfordernissen im Inneren variiert, sodass Bauten mit unterschied-lichem Charakter entstanden, was nicht zuletzt die Orientierung in der komplexen Anlage erleichtert. Viele Laborgruppen sind aller-dings Sicherheitsbereiche und nicht unbeschränkt zugänglich.

Optisch und formal zusammengefasst sind die verschiedenen Bau-körper durch die gemeinsame Architektursprache mit Anklängen an Aldo Rossis Typologien und an die Ästhetik der englischen High-Tech-Architektur. Mit silbern blinkenden Aluminiumblechfassaden, Tonnendächern (in denen sich die umfangreiche Haustechnik ver-birgt) und Lüftungskaminen geben sich die Bauten als Gehäuse für Labors und chemische Produktionsanlagen zu erkennen. Im Inneren sind sie überraschend wohnlich durch die ausgiebige Verwendung von Holz. Die Versorgung mit Medien geschieht bei den Labors von den Giebelseiten über die Flure, wodurch die Fensterflächen zur Belichtung gänzlich frei bleiben. In den Büros sorgen natürliche

The nine-storey, glazed atrium appears like an expansive gesture of welcome to the office building's visitors. Projecting considerably, the striking roof of the vestibule lends almost ceremonial gravity to any arrival by car. In the foyer, which is as high as a house, one can imagine just how many workers are busy behind the gallery balustrades. The foyer also represents the starting point of a central line through the company site, from which it is possible to access all the operational buildings.

When Gert Wingårdh joined the project in 1989, the pharmaceuticals manufacturer Hässle (later AstraZeneca) had already constructed a range of very different buildings on the new company site south of Göteborg. The subsequent task was to concentrate and supple-ment the site with a large number of new laboratory and technical buildings, and to unite these with the existing structures optically and operationally in order to create a functioning organism.

The new buildings have been added to the orthogonal layout pre-scribed by the existing structures—but they avoid a strict, mo-notonous line by alternating volumes oriented either longwise or crosswise. The building volumes vary in length and width according to their functional requirements, so that buildings with contrasting character emerge, which, not least, provide is an aid to orientation within the complex site. However, many groups of laboratories are security areas, not open to uncontrolled access.

The varying structural volumes are integrated optically and formal-ly by means of a shared architectural language that echoes both Aldo Rossi's typologies and the aesthetics of English high-tech architecture. The buildings are presented as fitting containers for laboratories and chemical production systems, with silver-shimmer-ing sheet aluminium façades, barrel roofs (in which the extensive house technology is concealed), and ventilation chimneys. Inside, they are surprisingly homely due to extensive use of wood. The delivery of material for the laboratories takes place from the gable sides, via the corridors: the window areas remain completely free

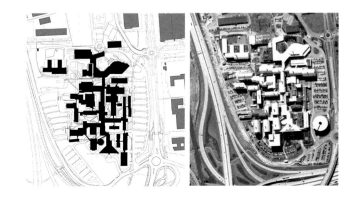

thermische Lüftungssysteme für Ventilation, wodurch abgehängte Decken vermieden werden konnten.

Eine andere Sprache als die technizistischen Labors spricht das Tagungs- und Restaurantgebäude im Süden. Die Konferenzräume einerseits und der große Restaurantbereich andererseits schmiegen sich in freier, polygonaler Grundrissorganisation um einen kleinen Hügel herum an die Felsen. Der lichte, hellgraue Raum des Restaurants gliedert sich in kleinere, kommunikative Gruppen auf verschiedenen Ebenen, als ob sich der Hügel im Inneren fortsetzte. Beton, Kalkstein und kanadisches Ahornholz bestimmen die warme, aber helle Atmosphäre des Hauses.

Das Betriebsrestaurant ist Ziel und Endpunkt des zentralen Erschließungswegs, eine gedeckte Passage durch das gesamte Firmengelände, die wie eine Schlagader mit abgehenden Nebenadern fungiert und als Verkehrs- und Begegnungszone gestaltet ist. Die Architekten nahmen sich die venezianischen Gassen zum Vorbild, die schmal sind und sich immer wieder aufweiten, immer neue Blickwinkel und Ausblicke eröffnen und trotz der Enge vielen Menschen Durchlass bieten. Kleine Aufenthaltsbereiche, ein Laden und Ausstellungsmöglichkeiten begleiten die Achse und bieten Gelegenheit, sich informell zu treffen. Die gemeinsamen Wege zum Ausgang und zum Lunch sollen die Kommunikation innerhalb des Betriebs fördern.

Als jüngstes Gebäude entstand neben der Vorfahrt ein andersartiger Bürobau, ein voll verglaster Block mit Sonnenschutzlamellen an der Südseite. In seinem Inneren hat ebenfalls das kommunikative Prinzip Vorrang, mit Großraum- und Gruppenbüros, einem großzügigen Angebot an Pausenflächen, mit Atrien, Brücken und offenen Treppenläufen. Durch dezente Farben und unauffällig gefärbte Gläser sind die Geschosse voneinander unterschieden. Auch in diesem lichtdurchfluteten, die perfekte Moderne zelebrierenden Bau finden sich die Materialien, mit denen der Architekt am liebsten arbeitet: blasser Kalkstein und warmes Holz.

to ensure maximum light. In the offices, ventilation is provided via natural thermal systems, avoiding suspended ceilings.

The conference and restaurant building in the south speaks a very different language to the technicised style of the laboratories. Here, the conference rooms and large restaurant area—with an open, polygonal ground plan—are set snugly against each side of a rocky hillock. The bright, light-grey space of the restaurant is divided into smaller, communicative group areas on different levels, as if the hill were continuing inside the building. Concrete, limestone and Canadian maple wood define the warm, bright atmosphere.

The company restaurant is the final destination on the central line of access: a covered passage through the whole site that functions like an artery with branching veins, also conceived as a circulation and meeting area. The architect's model was a Venetian alleyway, which is narrow in principle but frequently opens out to reveal new perspectives and vistas, and is passed through by so many people despite the confined space. Small break areas, a shop, and places for exhibitions are located along the axis, presenting opportunities to meet informally. The same route to the exit or lunch breaks is shared by all, as a tactic to promote communication within the company.

The most recent structure to be erected, beside the entryway, is a different kind of office building: a fully glazed block with sun-protection slats on the south side. Inside, the principle of communication is uppermost here as well, with open-plan and group offices, and a generous number of break areas with atriums, bridges, and open flights of stairs. The floors are differentiated by means of a restrained colour scheme and subtly toned glass. In this light-flooded building celebrating absolute modernity, it is also possible to find the materials with which Wingårdh prefers to work: pale limestone and warm wood.

Schwedische Botschaft, Berlin (DE)
Swedish Embassy, Berlin (DE)

Als sich die skandinavischen Länder 1995 zum Bau einer gemeinsamen diplomatischen Präsenz zusammentaten, war man sehr neugierig, wie diese Länder, die für kompromisslos moderne Architektur und schnörkelloses Design geschätzt werden, sich im traditionsbewussten Berlin verhalten würden. Vor dem Krieg reihten sich im Diplomatenviertel am Tiergarten Residenzen und Botschaften in Form von aufgeblasenen Villen mit herrschaftlichem Gestus. Der Krieg verschonte nur wenige dieser Häuser, doch als neuerlich Botschaften hier angesiedelt werden sollten, strebte der Senat von Berlin Respektierung der Historie des Quartiers, offene Bauweise mit Einzelgebäuden und Neubauten mit Villencharakter an.

Die fünf skandinavischen Länder allerdings beschlossen, in Berlin einen markanten gemeinsamen architektonischen Auftritt zu wagen. Sie entschieden sich beim Städtebauwettbewerb für die Arbeit der Wiener Architekten Alfred Berger und Tiina Parkkinen, die eine bislang in Berlin unbekannte Großform anboten, eine bandförmige, alle Botschaften mit dynamischem Schwung umfangende Kupferfassade, mit der die viergeschossigen Gebäude zu einer Familie vereint werden. Das Berliner Architekturbüro Pysall und Ruge wurde beauftragt, die gemeinsame Hülle und die fünf Siegerentwürfe der einzelnen Botschaftswettbewerbe sowie das gemeinsame „Felleshuset" mit zentralen publikumsintensiven Funktionen wie Kasino, Ausstellung und Veranstaltungssaal und gemeinsame Pforte zu realisieren.

Gert Wingårdh entwarf das Kanzleigebäude für die Schwedische Botschaft, 40 Arbeitsplätze und repräsentative Räume für den Botschafter. Die Wasserflächen zwischen den Botschaften erinnern zwar nicht in der Form, doch ideell an das alle verbindende Meer.

When the Scandinavian states collaborated to construct a joint diplomatic presence in Germany in 1995, there was much curiosity as to how these countries—admired for their consistently modern architecture and simple design—would conduct themselves in the tradition-conscious city of Berlin. Before the war a large number of residences and embassies, often pompous villas with a stately demeanour, were located in the diplomatic quarter beside the Tiergarten. The war spared few of those structures, but when the Berlin Senate decided to settle the city's embassies in the quarter once again, the declared intention was to respect the history of the area with open construction, separate buildings, and new embassies with "villa-character".

However, the five Scandinavian countries chose a striking, joint architectural presence in Berlin. An urban-developmental competition led to the success of Vienna architects Alfred Berger and Tiina Parkkinen, who suggested a large-scale precinct previously unknown in Berlin: a ribbon form enclosing all the embassies within the dynamic curve of a copper façade and uniting the four-storey buildings into one big family. The Berlin architectural office Pysall and Ruge was contracted to realise this joint "casing", the five winning designs in the individual embassy competitions, and the shared "Felleshuset" for functions involving the public—such as a casino, an exhibition and events hall, and the entrance gate.

Gert Wingårdh designed the chancellery building for the Swedish embassy to include forty work places and representative rooms for the ambassador. The areas of water between the embassies bring to mind the all-uniting sea—if not in their form, then at least as an idea. But we have to imagine the skerries ourselves when sit-

Die Schären muss man sich allerdings dazudenken, wenn man im Beratungszimmer der Schweden sitzt, das über dem Wasser zu schweben scheint. Der Architekt hat die im Gesamtplan angelegte Symbolik auf geistvoll abstrakte Weise übernommen. Drei Fassaden, drei Akte einer Inszenierung: Überlappend montierte schwarze Diabas-Platten aus Brännhult mit grobem Randschlag an der Westfassade sowie heller, feinbearbeiteter gotländischer Norrwange-Kalkstein und Opalglasplatten als Sonnenschutz an der Südseite bringen „schwedische Materialität" nach Berlin. Die gerundete Nord-Ost-Fassade vor der Glasfassade der Botschaft bildet die kupferne Außenhaut der Gesamtanlage, eine Schuppenwand aus grünen Lamellen, die mal vertikal geschlossen, mal horizontal durchsichtig oder in Zwischenstellungen montiert sind. Von innen leuchtet das warm-orange gebeizte Birkenholz hinaus, von außen wirkt das Grün des Tiergartens ins Haus.

Richard Serra gab die Inspiration für die gebogene Wand, die den Besucher ins Innere leitet. Freilich ist sie nicht aus rostigem Stahl, sondern aus dem von Wingårdh bevorzugten Kalkstein. Sie bildet die Innenwand des Beratungszimmers. Ein Teil von ihr kann als tonnenschwere Drehtür geöffnet werden.

Das Foyer, das sich als zentrale Halle in die Höhe entwickelt, strahlt in einem orange-braunen Holzton, der fast physisch Wohlbehagen verbreitet. Die Innenwände sind mit Birke verkleidet, ebenso die Wendeltreppe mit Kalksteinstufen und hölzernen Geländern in wunderbarer Handwerksarbeit. Der Balkon des Pausenbereichs und kleinere Besprechungszimmer schieben sich in verschiedener Höhe in die zentrale Halle und machen sie zu einem architektonisch abwechslungsreichen und komplexen Raum, von dem aus die drei Obergeschosse erschlossen sind.

Die einzelnen Büros sind an der West- und Südfassade in drei Geschossen aufgereiht. Der Botschafter waltet im südlichen Eckzimmer des dritten Obergeschosses seines Amtes.

Im Unterschied zu den nüchternen und raueren benachbarten Botschaften Finnlands und Norwegens bietet das schwedische Haus eine auf Anhieb sympathische Atmosphäre und offenbart auch in der Detaillierung außergewöhnliche handwerkliche Qualitäten.

ting in the Swedish consular offices, which seem to float in the air above the water. The architect has adopted the symbolism laid out in the overall plan in an intelligent, abstract way. The three façades are three acts in a dramatic production: "Swedish materials" are brought to Berlin by overlapping, rough-edged, black Diabas panels made of Brännhult on the west façade, whilst lighter, finely-worked Norrwange limestone from Gotland and opal-glass panels as sun protection are used on the south side. The curving north-east façade in front of the embassy's glass façade is formed by the external copper "skin" of the complete site. This is a scaled wall comprising green slats—some of which are closed vertical slats, some horizontal and transparent, and finally some fixed in intermediate positions. Birch wood stained in a warm orange tone glows from within, while the green of the Tiergarten seems to permeate the building from the outside.

Richard Serra provided the inspiration for the curving wall that leads visitors inside—although it is not made of rusted steel, but of the limestone that Wingårdh prefers. It also forms the inside wall of the consultation room. Part of it can be opened, courtesy of a revolving door that weighs a ton.

The foyer, which extends upwards as a central hall, glows in an orange-brown wood colour that radiates well-being in an almost physical way. The inner walls are clad in birch, and the spiral staircase with its limestone steps has beautifully hand-crafted wooden banisters. Smaller meeting rooms and the balcony of the staff recreation area project into the central hall at different heights, making it a diverse and complex architectural space from which the three upper floors are accessed.

Individual offices are lined up along the west and south façades, on three separate floors. The ambassador holds office in the corner room of the third floor, facing south.

By contrast to the sober, more severe style of the neighbouring Finnish and Norwegian embassies, the Swedish building generates an atmosphere that is immediately sympathetic, and outstanding qualities of craftsmanship are revealed in its details.

Ericsson European Headquarters, London (GB)

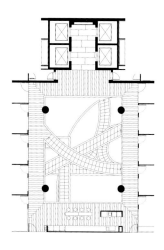

Das Eckgebäude am St. James's Square unweit des Piccadilly Circus hatte Ericsson als Neubau von einem Investor übernommen. Um die unspezifischen Büroflächen für die eigenen Zwecke zu qualifizieren und die Zusammenarbeit innerhalb des Hauses zu verbessern, erhielten Gert Wingårdh und Thomas Sandell den Auftrag, die Büros zu gestalten und den Innenhof zu einer Treppenhalle als Verbindungs- und Kommunikationszone umzubauen.

Angeregt durch ein Gemälde von Frank Stella schuf er eine labyrinthische Komposition aus geraden, gebogenen, gar geknickten Treppenläufen, die sich aus der Sicht von oben überlagern und überkreuzen und deutlich an die surrealen Treppen des M.C. Escher erinnern. Diese Treppenläufe scheinen, auch ohne begangen zu werden, ständig Kommunikationsströme durch den Raum zu schicken. Die weißen Brüstungen wirken wie Schienenwege mit den hölzernen Stufen als Schwellen.

Die Wirkung hat mit der archetypischen Reduzierung und der körperlichen Präzision zu tun. Treppenuntersicht und Geländer sind auf scharf geschnittene, weiße Flächen reduziert und bilden einen Trog, der im Kontrast dazu innen mit warmgoldenem Ahornholz ausgefüttert ist. Die Treppengeländer und die Brüstungen der Atriumgalerien haben identische Abmessungen und gehen nahtlos ineinander über. Verunsichernde Anschlussdetails gibt es nicht.

Abstrakte weiße Moderne da, wo Raum und Körper definiert werden, atmosphärisch empathische Holzoberflächen dort, wo der Mensch mit der Architektur unmittelbar in Berührung kommt: Das ist Wingårdhs Rezept, den Menschen intensive, angenehme Architekturerlebnisse zu vermitteln.

Ericsson took over the newly-built corner house on St. James's Square from an investor. It is situated not far away from Piccadilly Circus. In order to modify the unspecific office areas for its own purposes and to improve cooperation within the building, the company commissioned Gert Wingårdh and Thomas Sandell to redesign the offices and convert the inner courtyard into a stairwell that would serve as a circulation and communication area.

Stimulated by Frank Stella's paintings, they produced a labyrinthine composition of straight, curving, and even bending staircases that overlap and cross over one another when viewed from above—thus echoing the surreal staircases created by M.C. Escher. Even when they are not being used, these staircases seem to radiate constant streams of communication through the surrounding space. The white banisters resemble railroad tracks with the wooden steps as their sleepers.

The effect is dependent on the design's archetypical reduction and physical precision. From below, our perspective of the steps and banisters reduces them to sharply-cut, white geometric areas; they form a trough which is lined with contrasting warm, golden-coloured maple wood. The banisters and parapets of the atrium galleries have identical measurements and so merge seamlessly into one another: there are no disconcerting connecting details.

Abstract white modernism wherever space and volume are defined and atmospherically empathic wooden surfaces in those places where people come into direct contact with his architecture: this is Wingårdh's way of conveying an intense, pleasurable architectural experience to those people who use the building.

Villa Astrid, Hovås (SE)

Hovås gehört zu den Küstenorten südlich von Göteborg, die als naturnahe, privilegierte Wohngebiete geschätzt werden. Das Grundstück selbst ist weder großzügig noch besonders privilegiert, eher verwinkelt, die Aussicht aufs Meer Richtung Nordosten halb verdeckt durch den anstehenden Felsenhügel. Gert Wingårdh musste anders vorgehen als bei seinen Villen direkt am Wasser und ließ sich einen triangelförmigen Grundriss einfallen, der das Grundstück optimal ausnutzt.

Wieder arbeitet der Architekt mit dem Effekt der Überraschung. Der Besucher trifft auf eine niedrige, geschlossene, metallverkleidete Fassade mit nichts als einer Haustür, eingeklemmt zwischen den Felsen, in enger Nachbarschaft zu anderen Häusern. Erst im Inneren weitet sich das Haus, wird dreigeschossig, gibt den Blick frei auf einen geschützten Innenhof. Das Haus ist von oben nach unten entwickelt. Weil die Bauvorschriften die Traufhöhe auf 3,5 Meter beschränkten und eine Dachneigung von 14 bis 27 Grad vorschrieben, gräbt sich das Haus ein und erscheint von der Straße her eingeschossig. Mit seiner vorpatinierten Kupferfassade passt es sich den Felsen an und duckt sich vor dem Seewind.

Schlafzimmer und Fernsehzimmer liegen auf der unteren Ebene und sind zum eingetieften Atrium hin orientiert, in das Südwestlicht fällt. Der Tagesbereich mit Küche, Ess- und Wohnzimmer sowie der Bibliothek hat Ausblick zur See. Ein Studio ragt als Galerie in den Wohnraum und hat mit seinem großen Panoramafenster den besten Blick nach Westen. Der Westflügel mit seinem langen, flachgeneigten Dach klettert den Felshang hinauf. Am Südgiebel ist er bis auf den Fels hinab vollverglast. Im Inneren scheint der Fels unvermittelt durch das Fenster ins Haus zu stürzen. Grundwasser rinnt über den Granit und dringt als Naturelement ins Wohnzimmer ein. Entstanden ist auf engstem Grund und unter schwierigen räumlichen Verhältnissen ein erstaunlich geräumiges Haus, das mit Licht und Schatten, Aus- und Durchblicken spielt und während des Tageslaufs immer neue Architekturerlebnisse bietet.

Hovås, like many other coastal towns south of Göteborg, is highly rated as an elite residential district close to nature. The actual plot is neither extensive nor particularly favourable; in fact it is rather rambling, and its view of the sea to the north-east is half concealed by the adjacent rocky hillside. Gert Wingårdh had to adopt a different approach to that of his villas directly beside the water, and he conceived a triangular ground plan to exploit the site optimally.

Again, the architect worked with a surprise effect. Initially, in close proximity to other houses, the visitor encounters a low, closed, metal-clad façade caught between the cliffs, with nothing more than a door in it. But inside, the house expands over three storeys, opening up the view onto a sheltered inner courtyard. The layout of the house progresses from the top to the bottom. Because building regulations limited the height of the eaves to 3.5 metres and stipulated a roof incline of fourteen to twenty-seven degrees, the house is buried and appears to comprise only one floor from the street. The pre-patinated copper façade means that it is in keeping with the rocks and seems to duck down to avoid the sea wind.

The bedrooms and TV-room are on the lowest floor, oriented towards a sunken atrium that catches the light from the south-west. The day area with kitchen, dining room, living room, and library has a view towards the sea. A studio gallery extends into the living room; with its big panorama window, this area has the prime view to the west. The west wing with its long, gently sloping roof appears to climb up the slope of the cliff. The south gable is fully glazed down to the level of the rock. Inside, the rock apparently falls right through the window into the house. Ground water trickles over the granite and penetrates into the living rooms as an element of nature.

On the narrowest of sites and under difficult spatial conditions, the architect has produced an astonishingly spacious house that plays with light and shadow, views and vistas, and provides continually changing architectural experiences throughout the course of a day.

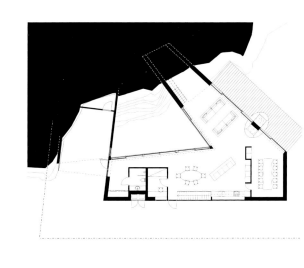

VillAnn, Särö (SE)

An der Westküste, 20 Kilometer südlich von Göteborg und damit noch im Einzugsbereich der Stadt, steht die VillAnn mit Blick nach Westen über Archipel und Kattegat, vom Ufer nur durch eine Erschließungsstraße getrennt. Wingårdhs jüngste Villa ist auch seine gestalterisch bislang diszipliniertieste und konsequenteste. Die Bauherren wussten genau, was sie wollten und hatten ein minimalistisches Haus geordert; Anlass für ihn, sich in formaler Reduktion zu üben und Gelegenheit, seinem vielgestaltigen Œuvre ein strenges, puristisches, einem Ideal angenähertes Artefakt hinzuzufügen. Und die Bauherren gaben sich perfektionistischer als so mancher Architekt – an Wingårdh erging der Auftrag, beim Bau des Hauses auf beste Sichtbetongüte zu achten.

Das Raumprogramm ist übersichtlich – Küche mit Nebenräumen, Esszimmer, Wohnraum im Erdgeschoss, zwei Zimmer im Obergeschoss – und ist linear im quergelagerten Baukörper organisiert. Die Giebelwände des Hauses sind zum Strand hin verlängert und umarmen die weitläufige Terrasse vor der gläsernen Westwand, die auf diese Weise in das Raumkontinuum des Hauses einbezogen wird. Bei sommerlichem Wetter sind die Grenzen des Innenraums zur Terrasse aufgehoben, man lebt drinnen und draußen, das Essen wird auf der langen Tafel unter einer stählernen Pergola serviert. Die einzelne Birke ist mehr schattenspendendes, architektonisches denn natürliches Element.

Vor der Terrasse bildet der Pool eine Abgrenzung wie ein Burggraben. Man kann ihn aber auch wie beim Barockschloss als Bassin im Vordergrund des Gartenparterres interpretieren. Das weitere Grundstück bis zur Straße ist von NOD Landschaftsarchitekten gestaltet worden, die bei ihrem Entwurf an stilisierte, geometrisierte Dünen gedacht haben. Beide Elemente haben die Aufgabe, das Haus gegen die Straße abzugrenzen, ohne diese Grenze materiell auszuformulieren.

Die Materialpalette ist äußerst reduziert. Das Haus besteht außen wie innen nur aus Sichtbeton und Glas sowie Böden und Einbau-

VillAnn is situated on the west coast twenty kilometres south of Göteborg and therefore still within the city's catchment area. With a view towards the west across the archipelago and the Kattegat, it is separated from the shore by no more than an access road. Wingårdh's most recent villa is also his most disciplined and consistent in design to date. The building clients knew exactly what they wanted and ordered a minimalist house, which gave the architect an opportunity to practise formal reduction and so add a strict, purist artefact—approaching an ideal—to his diverse oeuvre. The building clients handled themselves in a more perfectionist manner than many architects—commissioning Wingårdh to ensure that the best quality exposed concrete was used for the house's construction.

The arrangement of rooms is relatively simple—kitchen with auxiliary rooms, dining room, and living room on the ground floor, and two rooms on the upper floor—and organised in a linear way within the crosswise architectural volume. The gable walls of the house are extended towards the beach and enclose a spacious terrace in front of the glazed west wall, which is thus incorporated into the spatial continuum of the house. In summer weather, the barriers between interior and terrace are abolished; life takes place inside and out, and meals are served on the long table under a steel pergola. The single birch tree is more an architectonic feature to provide shade than a natural element.

In front of the terrace, the pool creates a boundary resembling a castle moat. However, it can also be interpreted as the basin between the ground floor and gardens of a baroque palace. The rest of the plot down to the road was designed by NOD landscape architects, who were inspired by the concept of stylised, geometricised dunes. The intention of both elements is to separate the house from the road without fully formulating a material boundary.

The range of materials is extremely reduced. Inside and out, the house consists of no more than exposed concrete and glass, with

möbeln aus Douglasienholz, das durch seine bleiche Lasur der Betonfarbe weitgehend angenähert ist. Die Trennwände zwischen Hauswirtschaftsbereich, Küche und Esszimmer werden von geräumigen Schrankwänden gebildet, die jegliche weitere Möbel unnötig machen. Wände, Tische und die Treppe nach oben sind in disziplinierte Reihe gebracht. Der Wohnraum aus drei Betonwänden, Betondecke und 14 Meter langen Dielen, und bar jeglicher Details, könnte puristischer nicht sein. Nur die Kaminnische ist Blickfang und natürlich die rahmenlose Glasfront nach Westen mit ihrem grenzenlosen Ausblick.

Wingårdh hat im Sinn Mies van der Rohes die Detailarbeit so weit getrieben, bis das Bauwerk auf seine reinen Grundelemente redu-

floors and fitted furniture made of Douglas fir—which has been approximated as closely as possible to the colour of concrete using a pale glaze. The dividing walls between the housekeeping area, kitchen, and dining room are formed by spacious cupboards that make any other kind of furniture superfluous. Walls, tables and the steps to the upper floor are set in disciplined rows. The living room is created by three concrete walls, a concrete ceiling, and fourteen-metre-long floorboards; with no details of any kind, it could not be more purist. Only the chimney corner catches the eye, as of course does the frameless glass front to the west with its endless view.

In the spirit of Mies van der Rohe, Wingårdh has taken the detail work so far that the construction seems to have been reduced to its

ziert erscheint, ungestört von allen vermeidbaren Fugen und Beschlägen, Sockeln und Leisten. Plötzlich wird der Beton zur edlen, idealisierten Oberfläche, werden zwei schlichte Pendelleuchten zum raumbildenden Element, wird ein Ruhesessel zum Schaustück. Der nüchterne, perfektionistische Rationalismus schlägt um in Poesie.

Indes, eine solche, dem Idealzustand entgegengetriebene Architektur der Moderne verträgt normalerweise keine Gebrauchsspuren. Der gepflegte Unterhalt des Hauses, auch die sparsam ausgesuchte Möblierung und einzelne, großformatige, in diesem Ambiente großartig zur Wirkung kommende Kunstwerke stellen jedoch unter Beweis, dass die Bewohner sich die Reduktionsästhetik bei ihrem Wohn- und Lebensstil zu eigen gemacht haben.

pure fundamental elements, undisturbed by avoidable joins and fitments, pediments, and borders. Concrete suddenly becomes a distinguished, idealised surface: two simple suspended lights develop into a space-creating element, and an armchair into a showpiece. Sober, perfectionist rationalism reverts to poetry.

As a rule, such modernist architecture striving for an ideal cannot tolerate any signs of use. But the neat maintenance of this house, including the sparse, select furnishings and isolated, large-format artworks—which produce a marvellous effect in this ambience—shows that the owners have made minimalist aesthetics into their style of life as well as décor.

Filippa K Ease Store, Stockholm (SE)

Ease ist eine neue Designlinie des schwedischen Labels Filippa K, die leger, weich, natürlich und komfortabel sein will. Trotz Hektik und Alltagsstress eins mit sich sein, sich wohlfühlen ist das Ziel, das die Kleidung unterstützen soll. Naturverbundenheit auf einer höheren, abstrakteren Ebene zur Wirkung zu bringen, war eine Vorgabe des Architekten für den Entwurf des neuen Label Stores in der Nähe des Östermalmtorg, beruhigte Atmosphäre und gedämpftes Farbspiel die andere. Modedesign ist von Farben dominiert und wechselt die Farbskala saisonbedingt zweimal im Jahr. Die Innenarchitektur eines Modegeschäfts unterliegt (normalerweise) längeren Erneuerungszyklen. Im Unterschied zu früheren Ladengestaltungen, die auf Formen, Farben und Effekte setzten, hat Gert Wingårdh für den Store der neuen Designlinie in der Fußgängerzone Grev Turegatan eine disziplinierte Architektur gewählt, die der saloppen Lebensart von Ease und auch der dezenten Herbstmode das Primat lässt.

Nur wenige, kubisch-blockhafte Möbel gliedern den Raum. Die in ein festes orthogonales Raumsystem eingebundenen Theken, Wände, Bänke und Regalnischen, alle Schreinerarbeiten und die Fußböden bestehen aus fahl gebeiztem Douglasienholz, das auch bei Effektbeleuchtung keine intensiven Farben ausstrahlt.

Natur ist unmittelbar präsent in Gestalt der Wand hinter der Theke, die in ganzer Höhe mit natürlichen Pflanzen bedeckt ist und das Klima im Store harmonisiert. Hinter der grünen Wand verbergen sich die Anprobekabinen. Bei dieser von der Gestaltung dominierten Arbeit steht Wingårdh in der Tradition des zurückhaltend auftretenden, naturnahen skandinavischen Designs.

The fashion line "Ease" designed by the Swedish label "Filippa K" aims to provide casual, soft, natural, and comfortable clothing. Its purpose is to convey a feeling of well-being, giving the wearers a sense of being at one with themselves despite the stressful pace of everyday life. One requirement of the architects designing the new label store close to Östermalmtorg was that they conjure close ties with nature on a higher, more abstract level; the other was to produce a tranquil atmosphere and muted play of colours. Fashion design is dominated by colours: their range is altered twice a year according to the season. The interior design of a fashion shop is subject (normally) to longer cycles of refurbishment. In contrast to his earlier shop designs accentuating forms, colours and effects, Gert Wingårdh therefore chose a disciplined architecture for the new line's store in the pedestrian precinct Grev Turegatan. It is a design that underlines the casual lifestyle of Ease and its restrained autumn fashions.

The space is divided by only a few cubic, block-like items of furniture. Counters, walls, benches, and shelf niches are incorporated into a strict orthogonal system, and all the carpentry work and the floors consist of pale-stained Douglas fir, which does not radiate intense colour even when lighting effects are employed.

Nature is immediately present in the design of the wall behind the counter, which is covered with natural plants to its full height and thus balances the climatic conditions in the store. The fitting rooms are concealed behind this green wall. In this work dominated by design, Wingårdh follows the tradition of apparently restrained Scandinavian design, close to nature.

Villa Nilsson, Varberg (SE)

Heftige Winde sind der Normalfall an der ungeschützten Westküste Hallands. Tief duckt sich das Haus zwischen die schützenden Felsen und Bäume, von der Straße aus fast unsichtbar. Man nähert sich von der Schmalseite her, tritt ins Halbdunkel des Foyers und überschaut das bergseitig von Oberlicht erhellte Haus in seiner ganzen Länge. Zum Wohnbereich im Zentrum des Raums hin senkt sich der Boden um sechs Trittstufen, um an der gegenüberliegenden Seite wieder anzusteigen. Einige Schritte hinab, und das Haus öffnet sich nach links mit einer atemberaubenden Aussicht nach Süden über das Kattegat.

Durch die wechselnden Raumhöhen und den Zuschnitt der Räume, aber auch über die Materialien ändert sich deren Charakter und Intimität. Gewachsener Fels tritt bis ins Innere des Hauses. Das Motiv wird von den gestaffelten Granittafeln in Eingangssituation und Wohnbereich auf abstraktere Weise wiederholt. Im Hintergrund führen drei Stufen auf die Ebene des Esszimmers und der Küche, deren Böden und Wände mit warmrotem Kirschholz bedeckt sind. Der Feuerplatz des Kamins zwischen Wohnbereich und Esstisch schwebt auf horizontalen Steintafeln und ist eingefasst von senkrecht gestellten Platten.

Die Schlafräume, ebenfalls mit wohnlichen Holzfußböden ausgestattet, sowie das mit Naturstein gestaltete Bad gliedern sich an der Bergseite an. Im Hintergrund endet der Flur an der Tür zu einem vom Seewind geschützten Gewächshaus am Westende des langgestreckten Gebäudes.

Nach Süden wird das Seepanorama zum Bauprogramm. Der Glasfront des Hauses auf ganzer Breite vorgelagert liegt die Terrasse mit leicht erhöhtem Essplatz. An der Ostseite befindet sich ein kleines Studio, das einer neugierig vorgeschobenen Aussichtskanzel gleicht. Senkrechte Granitscheiben umkleiden die Pfosten der Fensterfront, aus denen das Sonnenschutzdach herauswächst.

Strong winds are the norm on the unprotected west coast of Halland. The house is well tucked away between sheltering rocks and trees, almost invisible from the road. It is approached from the narrow end: one enters the semi-darkness of the foyer and is met by a view along the full length of the house, which is lit from above through skylights on the cliff side. The floor drops down six steps into the living area at the centre of this space, rising up again at the opposite side. A few steps down, and on the left the house opens out with a breathtaking view to the south across the Kattegat.

The changing heights and layout of the rooms, in addition to the materials used, influence their character and intimacy. Solid rock even permeates into the interior. This motif is repeated in a more abstract way by graduated granite slabs in the entry and living area. In the background, three steps lead to the level of the dining room and kitchen, the floors and walls of which are covered in a warm, red cherry wood. The fireplace between the living area and the dining table floats on horizontal stone slabs and is framed by vertical stones.

The bedrooms, also with homely wooden floors, and the bathroom designed in natural stone are arranged on the side facing towards the cliff. In the background, the hallway terminates in a door leading to the greenhouse at the western end of the elongated building, where it is protected from the sea winds.

To the south, the seascape provided the programme for building. The terrace has a slightly raised eating area and runs along the full width of the house's glass front. On the eastern side there is a small studio resembling a curiously projecting observation cockpit. Vertical slabs of granite clad the posts of the window front, and the sun-protection roof almost appears to grow out of them.

Again, Wingårdh begins a stylistic theme that is new to him, one that Modernism has been familiar with since the early twentieth

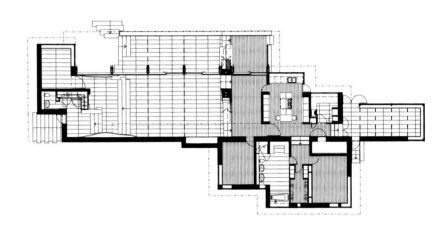

Stilistisch schlägt Wingårdh wieder ein für ihn neues Thema an, das die Moderne seit dem frühen 20. Jahrhundert kennt. Mit schwebenden Flächen, sich ablösenden Kuben und gestaffelten Wandscheiben betreibt er ein balancierendes Spiel mit Körper und Fläche, das an Gerrit Rietvelds De Stijl oder an Malewitschs und El Lissitzkys Suprematismus denken lässt. Über den erdverbundenen, organisch geformten Felsformationen schwebt deren künstliche Interpretation als geometrische Abstraktion. So schmiegt sich das Haus ganz eng an Natur und Landschaft und hebt sich doch davon ab als von menschlicher Hand geschaffenes Artefakt.

century. Using floating flat surfaces, sequences of cuboids, and graduated sections of wall, he plays a balancing game with volumes and flat surfaces reminiscent of Gerrit Rietveld's De Stijl or Malevich's and El Lissitzky's Suprematism. Above the earth-bound, organically formed rock formations, their artificial interpretation floats like a geometric abstraction. Thus the house, nestled snugly into the natural landscape, stands out from it as an artefact created by human hands.

Mühle, Västra Karup (SE)
Mill, Västra Karup (SE)

Das kleine Gebäude gehört zu einer Hofanlage aus dem späten 19. Jahrhundert mitten im südschwedischen Örtchen Västra Karup, die von Wingårdh zu einem Feriendomizil umgebaut worden war. Wo einst die Wassermühle stand, ergänzte er die Anlage um einen kleinen, delikaten Bau, ein zwischen Bäumen verstecktes Refugium, in das man sich zurückziehen kann. Das 50 Quadratmeter große Häuschen mit quadratischem Grundriss ist von archetypischer Einfachheit. Es durfte aus wasserrechtlichen Gründen nicht größer ausfallen als das ehemalige Mühlenhaus, das an dieser Stelle stand. Zwei der vier Wände sind massiv, zwei vollverglast ausgeführt.

Pate stand aber auch das japanische Teehaus, dessen Materialität und kontemplative Räumlichkeit und dessen intensiver Bezug zur Natur. Etwa das Spiel mit dem Wasser, das über steinerne Rinnen geführt wird, ein Tauchbecken zum Überlaufen bringt, sich auf einer Trittstufe verläuft, um dann in das künstliche Wasserbecken zu rinnen, das sich vor der schwebenden Terrasse ausbreitet. Der Pool wurde angelegt, weil das bescheidene Mühlbächlein oft zu wenig Wasser führt, um den Garten mit dem feuchten Element zu bereichern. Der ebenfalls japanisch inspirierte Garten wurde von NOD Natur Orienterad Design AB Stockholm gestaltet.

Gibt sich das Haus von außen schlicht und einfach, so entfaltet es im Inneren umso mehr gestalterischen Reichtum. Ein Wohnraum mit hängendem Kamin und eine kleine Küche nehmen den vorderen Teil des Raums ein, im Hintergrund liegen die Umkleidezone und die Sauna. Die Treppe an der rechten Giebelwand führt ins Dachgeschoss. Die Räume sind nicht durch Wände getrennt, sondern kaum merklich durch Niveausprünge von zwei Stufen.

Die warme Atmosphäre des Hauses wird vor allem durch das allgegenwärtige Eichenholz bestimmt. Ein stählernes „T" aus Doppel-T-Profilen trägt demonstrativ die als attraktives Raumelement präsente Holzbalkendecke. Alle Bauelemente, die Kalksteinfußböden wie die Holzeinbauten und die Möbel, sind sorgfältig detailliert und mit hoher Handwerkskunst gefertigt. So wurde das Haus zur Preziose, der bis ins letzte Detail die volle Aufmerksamkeit des Architekten zuteil wurde, wie es bei größeren Projekten kaum möglich ist.

This small building belongs to a late nineteenth century farm estate—converted by Wingårdh into a holiday home—located in the middle of the southern Swedish village Västra Karup. He added a small, delicate building to the site at the place where the watermill once stood: a refuge concealed among the trees. The little house measures only fifty square metres on a square ground plan; it is archetypal in its simplicity. Waterways regulations meant that it could not be any bigger than the mill-house that formerly stood on this spot. There are two massive stonework walls; the other two are completely glazed.

Another source of inspiration was the Japanese teahouse, with its materiality, contemplative space and powerful reference to nature. There is the play with water, for example, which is directed over stone rivulets, causing a basin to overflow and run onto a step—after which it flows into the artificial water pool laid out in front of the floating terrace. The pool was created because the modest mill stream is often not full enough to enhance the garden design with water as an element. Planned by NOD Natur Orienterad Design AB Stockholm, the garden also suggests a Japanese influence.

While the house conveys an impression of simplicity from the outside, a contrasting wealth of design is revealed inside. A living room with a suspended fireplace and a small kitchen take up the front area; at the back there is a place to change and the sauna. The stairs up the right-hand gable wall lead to the top floor. The rooms are not divided by walls but by subtle changes of level via two steps.

The house's warming atmosphere is generated mainly by oak, which is omnipresent. A steel "T" made of double T-profiles carries the wood-beam ceiling demonstratively; the beams are accentuated as an attractive spatial element. All the construction elements—the limestone floor as well as the oak fittings and the furniture—are meticulous in detail and products of top-quality craftsmanship. The house emerges as a gem, demonstrating the architect's full attention and personal devotion to the very last detail—something that is seldom possible in the case of bigger projects.

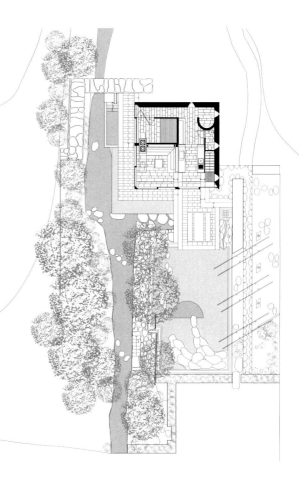

Hof Sand, Tofta Kungälv (SE)
Sand Farm House, Tofta Kungälv (SE)

Es ist das ideale Szenario, das man sich erträumt. Abseits des Betriebs, am Ende eines verschlungenen Wegs durch Fels und Heide: ein kleiner Hof in freier Natur. Zauberhafte Aussicht auf eine Bucht mit Schären, weiter Horizont, untergehende Sonne.

Gert Wingårdh erwarb 1992 ein kleines, 300 Jahre altes Bauernhaus, das zum Landgut Tofta gehört hatte. Die zusätzlichen Räume brachte er in zwei neuen Seitenflügeln mit Pultdach unter, wodurch sich ein geschützter Innenhof ergab. Der linke Flügel mit Verbindung zum Treppenhaus des Altbaus beinhaltet ein zentrales Wohnzimmer, zwei Schlafzimmer und ein Bad. Im rechten Flügel ist das Architekturbüro mit sechs Arbeitsplätzen untergebracht. Er steht nicht exakt im rechten Winkel zu den anderen Gebäuden, was der Baugruppe etwas Urtümliches, Gewachsenes gibt. Alt und Neu fügen sich zu einem Ensemble durch die im typischen Falunrot gestrichenen Holzfassaden mit gelb umrandeten Fenstern sowie die bewachsenen Torfdächer und sind doch mit einem Blick zu unterscheiden.

Wingårdh inszeniert in dem Haus auf beeindruckende Weise das Thema Schutz und Geborgenheit einerseits sowie Befreiung und Offenheit andererseits und spielt virtuos mit Lichtstimmungen und Atmosphären. Während man das Wohnzimmer – eigentlich eine Bibliothek, ringsum mit Bücherwänden, Lesetisch, Sofa und Sessel ausgestattet – als urgemütlich empfindet, überrascht nebenan das Esszimmer mit Lichtfülle und Offenheit. Die Wand zur Bucht hin besteht nur aus Glas, rahmenlos, ohne Sturz und Schwelle, ist optisch nicht vorhanden. Die anderen Wände, die Holzdecke, die Sitznische, die Polster und Kissen, ja selbst die Kunst an der Wand leuchten in einem satten Grün und machen das Zimmer zu einem eindrücklichen Farbraumerlebnis. Kernzelle des Hauses ist die nicht allzu große Küche, höhlenartig, bis zur Decke gefüllt mit Kochgerät, Geschirr und Vorräten und offenkundig intensiv im Gebrauch.

Bei schönem Wetter wird man sich zweifellos an der langen Tafel in der teilverglasten Loggia aufhalten mögen, die vor dem Wohnzimmer liegt und den freien Ausblick in die Natur geradezu zelebriert.

Die Aussicht ist auch die Attraktion im Schlafzimmer eine Treppe höher. Auch hier scheint die Wand zur Bucht hin zu fehlen, weil sie rahmenlos verglast ist: Man ist eins mit Himmel und Wetter. Auch

It is the ideal scenario—one that people dream about. Away from the stress of everyday life, at the end of a winding path through rocks and heather: a small farm estate in the midst of open countryside. A fantastic view onto a bay with skerries, a meadow leading down to the shore, a broad horizon, and the setting sun.

In 1992 Gert Wingårdh acquired a small 300-year-old farmhouse that had belonged to the estate of Tofta. He accommodated the additional rooms in two new side wings with single-pitch roofs, which led to the creation of a sheltered inner courtyard. The left-hand wing is connected to the stairwell of the old building and comprises a central living room, two bedrooms, and a bathroom. In the right-hand wing he accommodated his architectural office with six work places. This is not set at an exact right angle to the other buildings, giving the ensemble an original, naturally-developed aspect. The old and the new are united into an ensemble by means of wooden façades painted in the typical Falun red, windows outlined in yellow, and overgrown turf roofs—and yet they can be distinguished at a glance.

In the house, Wingårdh impressively stages the themes of shelter and safety on the one hand and freedom and openness on the other, playing brilliantly with moods of light and atmosphere. While the living room—actually a library with bookshelves all around, furnished with a reading desk, sofa, and armchairs—is perceived as extremely cosy, the adjacent dining room presents a surprising wealth of light and openness. The wall facing the bay consists purely of glass: frameless, with no sill or threshold, it has no optical presence. The other walls, the wooden ceiling, the seating niche, the upholstering and cushions, even the art on the wall gleam in a deep, dark green, and so make the room into an unforgettable colour experience. The heart of the house is the kitchen; although not terribly large, like a cave, it is filled to the ceiling with cooking equipment, crockery and supplies, and is obviously used intensively.

When the weather is fine, people will surely wish to spend time at the long table in the partially glazed loggia in front of the living room—a space that seems to preside over the view of the natural landscape.

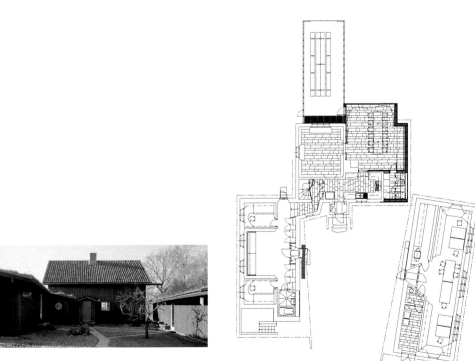

hier gibt es die alles kompromisslos beherrschende Einheitsfarbe für Wände, Decke und alle Einrichtungsgegenstände. Diesmal ist es Weiß. Wie das Esszimmer also ein ebenso überraschender, fast festlich wirkender Raum, durch die Dachflächen und schrägen Wände polygonal gebrochen, abstrakt modern und ohne jegliche Assoziation an Bauernhaus, Dachkammer, plüschige Gemütlichkeit.

Doch es gibt ja noch andere Farben. Der kleine Verbindungsflur und das Wohnzimmer im Seitenflügel strahlen in kräftigem Gelb, Wände und Decke im Badezimmer in Blau. Statt Fliesen kommt wieder der von Wingårdh favorisierte blass olivgrüne Kalkstein zum Einsatz, mit dem halbhoch die Wände, der Boden und die Badewanneneinfassung verkleidet sind.

Hof Sand ist der ideale Rückzugsort von der Hektik der Stadt, erholsam wie ein Ferienort, fast zu idyllisch, um hier auch zu arbeiten.

The view is also the attraction in the bedroom on the floor above. Here, too, the wall to the bay appears to be missing, since it is glazed and frameless: we are one with the sky and the weather. Here, too, there is a dominant colour for walls and ceiling, and for all items of furniture—with no compromise. This time it is white. Like the dining room, therefore, it is a surprising space that seems almost festive, broken up into polygons by the roof areas and sloping walls: abstract, modern, and triggering no associations whatsoever with a farmhouse, with attic rooms and plush cosiness.

But there are other colours: the small connecting corridor and the living room in the side wing glow with a strong shade of yellow, whilst thewalls and ceiling in the bathroom are blue. The pale olive green limestone favoured by Wingårdh is used again instead of tiles, cladding the walls to half-height as well as the floor and the skirting of the bathtub.

Sand Farm House is the ideal place to retreat from hectic urban life; with the same restorative effect as a holiday home, it is almost too idyllic to spend time working here.

Ale Kulturzentrum und Gymnasium, Nödinge (SE)

Ale Cultural Centre and Grammar School, Nödinge (SE)

Wie ein heruntergekommenes, unterprivilegiertes Stadtquartier aus den sechziger Jahren durch architektonische Interventionen wieder aufgewertet werden kann, veranschaulicht das Projekt in Nödinge. Neben dem schäbigen Einkaufszentrum, das bislang das Zentrum bildete, entstand ein Multifunktionsbau, der sich mit den Wohnungsbauten durch das gleiche Baumaterial, ein heller Klinker, verbindet. Die offene Schule mit ihrem vielfältigen Angebot an Bildungs- und Freizeitmöglichkeiten von der Bibliothek über Musik und Kunst bis zum Theater, vor allem für die Jugendlichen, hat das Quartier merklich stabilisiert. Das Gebäude, das sich in den Hügel duckt, lässt schon durch seine ungewöhnliche Dachform aufmerken. An der Stelle, wo das konkav geknickte Dach dramatisch fast bis zum Boden herabschießt, sollte man nicht ängstlich reagieren, alle Feng-Shui-Regeln vergessen und beherzt den darunter sich öffnenden Haupteingang durchschreiten.

Wer einen Schulflur erwartet hatte, wird überrascht, denn er steht in einem eindrucksvollen, ansteigenden Raum mit hölzerner Dachkonstruktion. Wie ein Weinberg staffelt sich die Bibliothek mit ihren Ebenen nach oben, ohne den Schematismus einschüchternder endloser Bücherreihen. Attraktiv und übersichtlich macht die Bücherei das erste Angebot, dem weitere folgen, rechter Hand der Theatersaal, links die Sport- und Veranstaltungshalle und der gleichzeitig als Foyer fungierende, mit Polsterbänken und Sitzgruppen bestückte große grüne Lichthof mit seinen Aufenthaltsmöglichkeiten. Von dröger Schulatmosphäre ist nichts zu spüren. Einige Schritte weiter ein zweiter, rot dominierter Lichthof, jener der Lehrer mit Lehrerzimmern und Verwaltung, dann der blaue, der „ruhige" Lichthof, auch er dreieckig und von zwei eingeschossigen Galerien umgeben.

Die Schule für 800 Schüler und die öffentlichen Funktionen sind eng miteinander verwoben. Der nördliche Trakt ist ein ehemaliger Teil des Einkaufszentrums, der umgebaut, in die Anlage integriert

The project in Nödinge shows how a rather shabby, under-privileged urban quarter from the sixties can be improved by means of architectonic interventions. A multifunctional building was erected beside the scruffy shopping mall that constituted the former centre and linked to nearby housing through use of the same building material—a light-coloured clinker brick. The open school offers various educational and leisure opportunities ranging from a library to music, fine art, and even a theatre. It is intended primarily for young people and has had a noticeably stabilising effect on the neighbourhood. The building is tucked into the hillside and draws immediate attention because of its unusual roof shape. At the place where the concave roof shoots dramatically almost to the ground, visitors should not react nervously, but forget all the rules of Feng Shui and walk boldly through the main entrance, which is located directly below this point.

Those expecting a school corridor will be surprised, since they are now standing in an impressive, ascending space with a timber roof construction. The library is graduated over rising levels like a vineyard, thus avoiding the regimentation of endless, intimidating rows of books. The attractive, easily comprehensible library is the first amenity available, but it is followed by others; on the right hand side there is the theatre auditorium, on the left a sport and events hall, and a large green atrium equipped with padded benches and seating groups. This is intended as a recreation area, but also functions as a foyer. There is no suggestion of listlessness. A few steps further on, dominated by the colour red, a second atrium accommodates the teachers' facilities including staffrooms and administration offices, and then there is the quiet, blue atrium—triangular in shape and surrounded by two single-storey galleries.

The school for 800 pupils and the complex's public functions are closely interwoven. The northern wing was formerly part of the

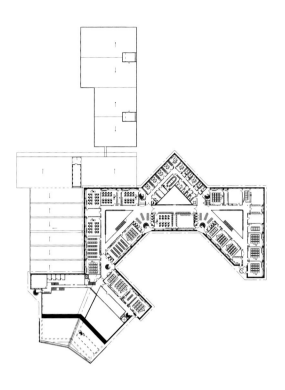

wurde und ein Zentrum für Erwachsenenbildung, die Mensa und Studios für Medienkurse aufnahm.

Vielleicht liegt es an den abwechslungsreichen, mal engen, mal weiten, mal übersichtlich hellen und mal dunkleren, heimeligeren Räumlichkeiten, vielleicht an den einfachen, durchaus robusten Materialien, vielleicht an der sympathischen, in Gelbtönen changierenden Farbpalette des von der Holzkonstruktion und Ziegelwänden dominierten Gebäudes, jedenfalls wird das Haus von seiner nicht unproblematischen Klientel gut angenommen. Durch die bewusst ökologische Bauweise mit dauerhaften Materialien und mit einem besonderen Augenmerk auf ein natürliches Lüftungssystem mit großen Querschnitten sollte ein gesundes, nachhaltiges Gebäude entstehen. Auch nach Jahren intensiven Gebrauchs zeigt es sich in guter Verfassung und seiner Aufgabe gewachsen.

shopping mall, which has been converted and integrated into the complex and now accommodates an adult education centre, the cafeteria, and studios for media courses.

Perhaps because of the great variety of rooms (some narrow and some wide, some clear and bright, and some darker and cosy), perhaps because of the simple and certainly robust materials used, or perhaps due to the sympathetic range of colours with variable shades of yellow in a building dominated by its wooden construction and brick walls—whatever the reasons, the complex has been well-received by its occasionally problematic clientele. The aim was to create a healthy, sustainable structure with enduring materials, using consciously ecological building methods and paying special attention to a natural ventilation system with ample cross-sections. Even after years of intense use, the centre still fulfils its purpose in an exemplary way and remains in excellent condition.

Villa Roser, Skara (SE)

Flachgieblige Einfamilienhäuser wie aus dem Katalog am Rand der alten Bischofsstadt Skara bilden die Umgebung. Am Ende der Straße ein anderes Bild: Vor dem Hintergrund mächtiger Laubbäume eine holzverkleidete Fassade, die sich beim Näherkommen zu einer Komposition aus zwei quer übereinandergelegten Kuben entwickelt. Das Haus schafft sein eigenes Ambiente, orientiert sich nach Westen, wo sich die Aussicht auf das Flüsschen und die parkartige Umgebung eröffnet.

Die Kuben formen gleichzeitig mit einfachen Mitteln die Außenräume, den Vorplatz, die Terrasse, den Balkon vor dem Obergeschoss. Eine Lamellenwand markiert den Eingang; das Garagentor ist als solches nicht erkennbar, sondern verschwindet in der Struktur der Wandverkleidung.

Der erste Eindruck im Inneren: genügend Platz im Entree für alles, was eine vierköpfige Familie an Winterkleidung und Utensilien ins Haus bringt. Linker Hand die offene Küche und der Blick in den Wohnbereich. Wenige Materialien bestimmen den Raumeindruck: der lebhaft graurot gemusterte Naturstein aus der Region, das

The setting on the edge of the old bishop's city of Skara is defined by low gabled, detached houses that could have come straight from a catalogue. But a different picture is painted at the end of the street: a timber-clad façade set against a background of massive deciduous trees, which—as one comes closer—emerges as two cubes placed at right angles, one above the other. The house creates its own ambience; it is oriented towards the west, where the view opens onto a small river and park-like surroundings.

The cubic volumes employ simple means to define the exterior— the forecourt, the terrace, and the balcony on the upper floor. A wall of slats marks the entrance, where it is impossible to recognise the garage door as such, because it disappears into the structure of the façade's cladding.

Inside, the first impression in the entry area is one of space— enough to store everything that a family of four may bring into the house in the way of winter clothes and equipment. On the left there is the open-plan kitchen and a view into the living area. Only a few materials define our impression: striking natural stone from

Eichenparkett, die hell lasierten Holzwände. Sie lassen erahnen, dass das ganze Haus, auch in seinen konstruktiven Teilen, aus dem nachwachsenden Rohstoff gebaut ist. Die offene Küche und das Wohnzimmer nehmen den einen Flügel ein, Bad und Schlafzimmer den anderen. Der in warmen Farben changierende Naturstein ist für die Stimmung im Bad verantwortlich, die an eine Naturtherme erinnert. Besonderer Clou ist die Badewanne, die versenkt in einem gläsernen Erker vor der Fassade liegt und ein Badeerlebnis mit Naturblick verspricht.

Eine schmale hölzerne Treppe führt ins Obergeschoss mit den Kinderzimmern, einem weiteren Wohnbereich und einer Sonnenterrasse, die durch den Rücksprung des Baukörpers über dem Erdgeschoss entsteht.

Geheizt wird das nach ökologischen Kriterien konzipierte Haus mit Erdwärme aus einer 120 Meter tiefen Bohrung.

Insgesamt kann das Haus als Neuinterpretation der eleganten Villenkultur der zwanziger Jahre unter den heutigen Voraussetzungen gesehen werden.

the region, patterned in red and grey, an oak parquet floor, wooden walls stained in a light-coloured varnish. One assumes that the whole house is constructed from this renewable raw material. An open-plan kitchen and living room take up one wing, the bathroom and bedrooms the other. The atmosphere in the bathroom, reminiscent of a natural spa, is created by natural stone with its shimmering warm colours. The sunken bath tub itself is a special attraction, as it is located in a glass bay area projecting from the façade and promises a bath-time experience with a marvellous view of the countryside.

A narrow wooden staircase leads to the upper floor with children's rooms, a second living area, and a sun terrace that is created by the receding volume of the building above the ground floor.

The house's heating system was planned according to ecological criteria and functions using geothermal energy from a bore hole 120 metres deep.

All in all, the house can be seen as a reinterpretation of twenties villa culture from the premises of contemporary architecture.

Schwedisches Haus, Washington DC (USA)
House of Sweden, Washington DC (USA)

Sie ist nicht nur eine der offensten Botschaften in der amerikanischen Hauptstadt, an einer stark frequentierten Uferpromenade am Zusammenfluss von Rock Creek und Potomac River vom Regierungsviertel nach Georgetown gelegen, sie ist auch das Informations- und Kulturzentrum des nordischen Landes und wird deshalb „Schwedisches Haus" genannt. Das Haus reagiert auf die urbane Situation, öffnet sich den Passanten, um ihnen von Schweden zu erzählen. Ohne Behinderung durch Zaun oder Mauern können sie einen neugierigen Blick in das gläserne Erdgeschoss werfen oder gleich eintreten, um Ausstellungen oder Veranstaltungen zu besuchen. Wohnungen und Dachterrasse gehören zu den für ein Botschaftsgebäude ungewöhnlichen Ausstattungen, wodurch das Schwedische Haus in großen Teilen für Menschen zugänglich ist, die nicht der Botschaft angehören.

Wingårdh hat einen Zugang inszeniert, der die Erwartungshaltung steigert. Zwei Wasservorhänge der Glasdesignerin Ingegerd Råman begrenzen den schmalen Weg. Eine Rampe entlang der Westseite führt zur Schmalseite des Gebäudes am Flussufer. Dort liegt der Eingang in das hinter die Stützen zurückgezogene gläserne Foyer und die Ausstellungsräume. Auf der unteren Ebene mit Ausblick zum Rock Creek führt eine Wasserrinne aus schwarzem Marmor durch die Glaswand bis in ein Becken unter der Haupttreppe.

Der Vortragssaal und mehrere Sitzungszimmer der Veranstaltungsebene im Untergeschoss ergänzen das öffentliche Angebot des Schwedischen Hauses. Das erste Obergeschoss ist der Kanzlei der Botschaft mit 40 Einzelbüros und den Räumen des Botschafters vorbehalten. Darüber liegen zwei Geschosse mit 20 Apartments und auf dem Dach eine Terrasse mit traumhaftem Ausblick auf das Kennedy Center, die Key Bridge, Roosevelt Island und den Potomac hinab bis zum Pentagon.

It is not only one of the most open embassies in the American capital, at the point where Rock Creek meets the Potomac River on a busy waterside promenade from the government district to Georgetown; it is also the Nordic country's information and cultural centre and therefore known as the "House of Sweden". The building responds to the urban situation, opening up to passers-by to tell them about Sweden: unhampered by fencing or walls, they can satisfy their curiosity by taking a look into the glazed ground floor or simply walking right in to visit exhibitions or events. Apartments and a roof terrace are features not usually encountered in embassy buildings; they mean that much of the House of Sweden is accessible to people who do not belong to the embassy staff.

Once again, Gert Wingårdh has staged an entrance that heightens our expectations. Two curtains of water created by glass designer Ingegerd Råman mark the narrow entranceway. A ramp along the west side leads to the narrow end of the building on the river bank. There, set back behind supports, is the entrance to a glazed foyer and the exhibition rooms. On the lowest level looking out over Rock Creek a rivulet of black marble leads water through the glass wall into a basin below the main staircase.

The lecture hall and several meeting rooms on the events level in the basement complete the facilities that the House of Sweden offers to the public. The first floor is reserved for the embassy chancellery with forty individual offices and the ambassador's rooms. Above this there are another two floors with twenty apartments and a roof terrace with a magnificent view to the Kennedy Center, Key Bridge, Roosevelt Island, and down the Potomac to the Pentagon.

As a direct consequence of the shape of the plot, the building's ground plan is a parallelogram. All floors have a central access zone that culminates in a glazed stairwell at the north gable. Balcony

Der Zuschnitt des Grundstücks führte zu einem parallelogrammförmigen Grundriss des Gebäudes. Die Geschosse haben eine mittlere Erschließungszone, die am Nordgiebel in einem gläsernen Treppenturm endet. Die blockhafte Grundform wird aufgelöst durch den umlaufenden Balkonerker vor den beiden Wohnetagen.

Durch Glas, Marmor, Holz und Lichtpunkte sollen die schwedischen Elemente Wasser, Eis, schwarze Nacht und weißer Schnee architektonisch ausgedrückt werden. Im Unterschied zum Kanzleigeschoss, das mit vor der Marmorfassade schwebenden, transparenten Glasplatten verkleidet ist, sind die Glasscheiben der Balkonbrüstungen mit einem Dekor bedruckt, das Ahornfurnier darstellt. Wingårdh bezieht sich auf die schwedische Tradition der Imitationsmalerei, wie sie in historischen Häusern im Stockholmer Freilichtmuseum Skansen zu sehen ist. Am Abend glüht und leuchtet die von innen illuminierte „Holzfassade" wie Nordlicht weithin über den Fluss.

An der Eingangstür beeindruckt den Besucher zunächst ein aus dem vollen Holz geschnitzter Türgriff. Im Inneren bestimmt dann echtes Holz die für eine moderne Raumgestaltung ausgesprochen warme Atmosphäre. Wände und Decken sind mit hellem amerikanischen Ahornholz bekleidet und künden von der Tradition schwedischer Holzbauweisen. Die Inneneinrichtung ist von hohem handwerklichen Standard. Die Botschaftsräume im Obergeschoss wurden mit schwedischen Klassikern möbliert.

Elegantes Design, der Umgang mit Holz, Perfektion, Solidität und Wertarbeit, aber auch Offenheit und Gastfreundschaft, all die schwedischen Werte werden vom Schwedischen Haus in Washington eindrucksvoll präsentiert.

bays along the entire front of the two residential floors break up the basic block-like form.

The concept was to express in architecture the typical Swedish elements of water, ice, black night, and white snow using glass, marble, wood, and spots of light. By contrast to the chancellery floor, which is clad in transparent glass planes that seem to float in front of the marble façade, the glass of the balcony balustrades is printed with a décor suggesting maple wood veneer. This artificial heightening of the wood décor is Wingårdh's reference to the Swedish tradition of wood-imitation painting, which can be seen in historic houses at the Stockholm open-air museum Skansen, for example. In the evenings, this "wooden façade" is back-lit so that it glows and shimmers across the river like northern lights.

At the entrance, visitors are impressed immediately by a door handle carved from solid wood. Inside, real wood also defines the atmosphere, which is extremely warm for a modern spatial design. Walls and ceilings are clad in pale-coloured American maple wood, proclaiming the tradition of Swedish wooden building methods. The craftsmanship of the interior fittings is extremely high-quality. The embassy rooms on the first floor are furnished with classic Swedish furniture.

All the Swedish values—elegant design, expert handling of wood, perfection, solidity, and quality craftsmanship, along with openness and hospitality—are demonstrated most effectively by the House of Sweden in Washington.

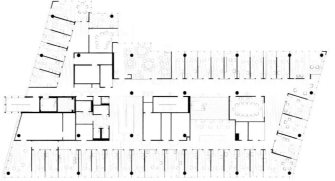

MITARBEITER
COLLABORATORS

Mitarbeiter Collaborators
Ulrika Ahlberg, Therese Ahlström, Mikael Andersson, Tove Andrée, Lars Anfinset, Leila Atlassi, Mats Bengtsson, Johan Berg, Claes Berglöf, Ewa Bialecka-Colin, Christine Björkman, Magnus Börjesson, Lena Centerwall Arthur, Jeannette Cervell, David Christofferson, Kima Ciftcioglu, Traian Cimpeanu, Vanessa D'Hooge, Dan Danielsson, Ulrika Davidsson, Pedro De Sousa E Brito, Nisani Demirel, Jonas Edblad, Peter Ejvegård, Johan Eklind, Charlotte Erdegard, Pål Ericksson, Lena Fagle, Tobias Fasth, Susanne Flinck, Carina Frickeus, Daniel Frickeus, Ola Frödell, Christophe Ginguene, Per Glembrandt, Tuva Gotte, Fredrik Gullberg, Lennart Gullberg, Ingrid Gunnarsson, Jannika Gustafsson Wirstad, Anne Gustavsson, Foued Hajjam, Chaker Halila, Kajsa Halldén, Pär Hedefält, Sara Helder, Bengt Hellsten, Robert Hendberg, Andreas Henriksson, Anna Höglund, Maria Ivarsson, Liselott Jademyr, Rickard Karlsson, Josefine Kastberg, Karolina Keyzer, Konrad Krupinski, Taito Lampinen, Kia Larsdotter, Josefin Larsson, Pilutaq Larsen Ström, Andreas Lindblom, Jakob Luttinger, Fredrik Lyth, Joakim Lyth, Maria Lyth, Petter Lyth, Jannice Magnusson, Vendela von Malmborg, Camilla Magnusson, Camilla Maruyama, Anna Mitrolios, Ry Morrison Romero, Gunilla Murnieks Andersson, Madeleine Müller Lightner, Sven Nejstgaard, Danuta Nielsen, Stefan Nilsson, Björn Nilsson, Fredrik Nilsson, Maria Normann, Anna Nyborg Lafveskans, Thomas Ocklund, Per Odebäck, Peter Öhman, Anders Olausson, Maria Olausson, Sebastian Olsson, Anna Palm, Monika Pitura, Alexandra Pripp, Fredrik Prytz, David Regestam, Filip Rem, Per Riihiaho, Susanna Ringnér, Charlotta Rosell, Mikael Rücker, Hanna Samuelsson, Pieter Sierts, Julia Steffensen, Sören Steffensen, Anna Stenberg, Birgitta Stenvaller, Paula Stenqvist, Madeleine Stoops, Henrik Strandhede, Cecilia Ström, Anna Sunnerö, Helena Toresson, Alice Van, Katarina Vukoja, Rasmus Wærn, Martina Wahlgren, Viktoria Wallin, Elin Wallinder, Frida Wallner, Johan Wegbrant, Gert Wingårdh, Karin Wingårdh, Maria Zalecka, Jacek Zalecki

Ehemalige Mitarbeiter Previous Collaborators
Pia-Cally Ahlgren, Håkan Albeman, Leila Alves-Bonnier, Anna-Karin Andersson, Elin Andreassen, Gustav Appell, Anna Artelius, Lennart Assmundsson, Jörgen Backman, Idun Bäck, Eva Bähr-Turndal, Anna Barne, Claudius Bäuerle, Kia Bengtson, Sanna Bergman Svärd, Ulrika Bergström, Martin Bergqvist, Elin Björling, Fabian Blücher, Lisbeth Bohman, Jenny Bornstein, Åke Boustedt, Louise Brant Lövenstierner, Peter Bringselius, Inger Broberg, Anneli Carlsson, Annika Carlsson, Johan Casselbrant, Claude Christensson, Christine Cleve Aponno, Kajsa Crona, Astrid Cronwall, Göran Dalhov, Stefan Dallendorfer, Aron Davidsson, Pawel Druciarek, Björn Dufva, Josef Eder, Torbjörn Edgren, Georg Edström, Kristoffer Ek, Monica Ekblom, Jonas Eliasson, Pär Eliasson, Elin Emsheimer, Anders Enerbäck, Mats Ericsson, Eva Eriksson, Karin Eriksson-Belart, Ulrika Eriksson, Caroline Fernfors, Anna Figelius, Mikael Frej, Niclas Frenning, Christian Frisenstam, Joel From, Markus Furby, Emma Görander, Oskar Götestam, Maria Grunditz, Nils Gulin, Kristofer Gullberg, Sarah Gunnarsson, Pierre Håkansson, Jan Hammargren, Tomas Hansen, Linda Hansson, Per Hansson, Linda Hedin, Jessica Hedlund, Ulf Hellsten, Helena Hemminger, Susanne Hodne, Cecilia Hörngren, Monica Horniak, Gustav Hult, Dan Idehed, Johan Israelsson, Anna Järvenpää, Jenny Johansson, Kajsa Johansson, Roger Johansson, Gabriella Jonsson, Joakim Juel, Joakim Kaminsky, Erik Kampman, Magnus Kardborn, Paula Karlander, Emma Karlsson Bruhn, Emma Kaudern, Harald Keijer, Fredrik Kihlman, Ola Kjellander, Henrik Kjellberg, Fredrik Kjellgren, Vera Knihova, Vanja Knocke, Jerry Kopare, Taiga Koponen, Nils Korth, Carina Krantz, Shamiram Kucukkaplan, Karin Larsson, Linnea Larsson, Karolina Leijonberg, Petter Leyman, Markus Lidfeldt, Hanna Lidström, Carina Lind, Ingegerd Lind, Daniel Lindberg, Jessica Lindblad, David Lindecrantz, Carola Lindholm, Germund Lindunger, Erik Linn, Anna-Klara Lövenberg, Tomas Lundberg, Torbjörn Lundell, Hanna Lundén, Mia Lundin, Anders Lundqvist, Andreas Lyckefors, Erik Magnusson, Chatarina Malmquist, Henrik Markhede, Erik von Matern, Klas Moberg, Bo Molander, Molly Möller, Pierpaolo Moramarco, Linda Näslund, Olle Netzell, Ulrik Neuendorf, Trung Nguyen-Viet, Jesper Nilsson, Milott Nilsson, Patrik Nilsson, Torgny Nordin, Josefina Nordmark, Johan Norén, Bitte Nygren, Åsa Nyvall, Anna Odlinge, Leif Ödman, Ann Olausson, Catrin Olsson, Anna Ornered, PO Oskarsson, Stefan Ostrowski, Andreas Pehrson, Birgitta Persson, Martin Persson, Fredrik Pettersson, Rikard Pettersson, Keimann Pham, Anna Pihl, Jennifer Pihl, Urban Pihl, Filippa Pyk, Jens Ragnarson, Anders Ränk, Anna Rehdin, Tobias Rosberg, Jacob Rose, Kristoffer Roxbergh, Christian Rusch, Alexandra Rylander, Jacob Sahlqvist, Nina Salomonsson, Yvonne Schmidt, Henrik Schulz, Anneli Selling, Mike Shanahan, Stefan Sjöberg, Johanna Sjögren, Sven-Magnus Sjögren, Mikael Sonnsjö, Sara Sotujo, Leon de Sousa E Brito, Paula Stålfors, Helena Stangenberg, Martin Steen, Smajo Stender, Andreas Stålnacke, Katarina Sundén, Christine Svensson, Tove Svensson, Per Söderberg, Tord-Rikard Söderström, Poul Erik Sörensen, Solveig Sörman, Ulf Thorbjörnsson, Caroline Timbré, Raymond Tollbom, Lena Tormund, Svante Wagenius, Mathias Wagmo, Anna Wallerstedt, Walter Wangler, Jan Vasilis, Lotta Wennerberg, Henric Wernefeldt, Lotta Werner Flyborg, Susann Wessely, Henrik Wibroe, Greger Wierusz, Josefine Wikholm, Anders Wilhelmson, Jens Vilhelmson, Erik Williamsson, Annika Wingårdh, Marikka Wingårdh, Rasmus Wingårdh, Tomas Voghera, Niklas Zetterberg, Wanda Zubillaga

Gert Wingårdh

Gert Wingårdh

Prof. MA., geboren 1951 in Skövde, studierte an der Technischen Universität Chalmers in Göteborg, wo er 1975 den Master of Architecture erwarb. 1975 trat er in Olivegrens Arkitektkontor AB ein, zwei Jahre später machte er sich selbstständig.

Bis 1978 firmierte das Büro AOW Assmundsson Ostrowski och Wingårdh Arkitekter och Samhällsvetare AB in Partnerschaft mit Lennart Assmundsson und dem Soziologen Stefan Ostrowski. 1978–85 Wingårdh & Wingårdh Konsulter HB in Partnerschaft mit Annika Wingårdh, 1985–88 Wingårdh & Wingårdh & Wilhelmson in Partnerschaft mit Annika Wingårdh und Anders Wilhelmson, 1988–90 Wingårdh & Wingårdh AB und schließlich seit 1990 Wingårdh Arkitektkontor AB. Das Zweigbüro in Stockholm wurde 1985 eröffnet.

Gert Wingårdh lehrt an der Technischen Universität Chalmers in Göteborg und ist seit 2000 Vorsitzender des Lenkungsausschusses des Fachbereichs Architektur. Er ist seit 1992 Mitglied der Königlichen Akademie der Schönen Künste, war von 1997 bis 2005 Vorstandsvorsitzender des Schwedischen Architekturmuseums und ist seit 1999 Mitglied der Königlichen Akademie des Ingenieurwesens und der Wissenschaften. Er erhielt mehrmals den renommierten Kasper Salin Preis.

Prof. MA., born in Skövde in 1951, he studied at Chalmers University of Technology in Göteborg, where he acquired his Master of Architecture in 1975. In 1975 he joined Olivegrens Arkitektkontor AB, and set up his own business two years later.

Until 1978 the office operated under the name AOW Assmundsson Ostrowski och Wingårdh Arkitekter och Samhällsvetare AB in partnership with Lennart Assmundsson and the sociologist Stefan Ostrowski; from 1978–85 as Wingårdh & Wingårdh Konsulter HB in partnership with Annika Wingårdh; from 1985–88 as Wingårdh & Wingårdh & Wilhelmson in partnership with Annika Wingårdh and Anders Wilhelmson; from 1988–90 as Wingårdh & Wingårdh AB and, finally, from 1990 onwards as Wingårdh Arkitektkontor AB. The branch office in Stockholm was opened in 1985.

Gert Wingårdh teaches at Chalmers University of Technology in Göteborg and has been chairman of the steering board of the architectural section since 2000. He has been a member of the Royal Academy of Fine Arts in Sweden since 1992; from 1997–2005 he was chairman of the board of the Swedish Museum of Architecture, and since 1999 he has been a member of the Royal Academy of Engineering and Sciences. Wingårdh has been awarded the well-known Kasper Salin Prize on several occasions.

VIERZEHN FRAGEN
FOURTEEN QUESTIONS

Falk Jaeger (FJ) Wie sind Sie zum Architekten geworden?

Gert Wingårdh (GW) Ich habe 1971 in Göteborg an der Technischen Universität Chalmers das Architekturstudium aufgenommen und hier 1975 auch das Diplom gemacht. Mein wichtigster Lehrer war Professor Jan Wallinder. Ich wollte dann zunächst ins Ausland gehen, nach England, der Sprache wegen. Ich habe bei Foster, Rogers und Stirling angefragt, aber die Zeiten waren schlecht, und es war schwierig, einen Job zu bekommen. Und mein Sohn wurde geboren, zu früh, in der 27. Woche; mit ihm auf dem Rücken wollte ich nicht nach England gehen. Ich bekam eine Anstellung im Büro eines meiner Professoren an der Chalmers, Johannes Olivegren, bei dem ich zweieinhalb Jahre blieb und viele Wettbewerbe absolvierte. Ich arbeitete auch an drei Projekten mit Jan Wallinder. 1977 bekam ich die Gelegenheit, eine Villa zu entwerfen. Meine Frau verdiente damals viel mehr Geld als ich und so konnte ich die Anstellung aufgeben und die Villa bauen. Damit eröffnete ich mein Büro. Es kam rasch eine weitere Villa, dann einige Interieurs, die in den achtziger Jahren zu weiteren Interieurs, zu Restaurants und Läden führten …

Falk Jaeger (FJ) Who were the teachers that shaped you during your education?

Gert Wingårdh (GW) In 1971 I began studying architecture at Chalmers Technical University in Göteborg, where I also completed my diploma in 1975. The most important teacher for me was Professor Jan Wallinder. Initially, I wanted to go abroad after that—to England, because of the language. I made some enquiries with Foster, Rogers and Stirling, but times were bad and it was difficult to get a job. And then my son was born, too early, in the twenty-seventh week of pregnancy; I didn't want to go to England carrying him around on my back. I got a job in the office of one of my professors at Chalmers, Johannes Olivegren, where I remained for two and a half years. During that time we completed several competition entries. I also worked on three projects with Jan Wallinder. In 1977 I was given the opportunity to design a villa. At that time my wife was earning far more than I was, so I was able to give up my job and build the villa. That was how I opened my office. Another villa came along quite quickly, and then some interiors, which led to more interiors, restaurants and shops in the eighties …

I entered the first competition on my own behalf in 1974, and the only remarkable thing

Meinen ersten eigenen Wettbewerb machte ich 1974, bei dem das einzig Bemerkenswerte war, dass ich einen siebten Preis mit Sigurd Lewerentz teilte!

1982 hatte ich den ersten Angestellten. 1983 bekam ich den Auftrag, ein altmodisches Hotel in Malmö neu zu gestalten. Das absolvierte ich mit dem Schwerpunkt auf handwerklicher Qualität, wie es damals in Schweden nicht üblich war. Das führte zu einem Anschlussauftrag für das Hilton Slussen in Stockholm. Es begann eine Zeit des Reisens zwischen Göteborg und Stockholm, denn mit dem Auftrag eröffnete ich dort 1985 ein Zweigbüro. 1988 bekamen wir den Kasper Salin Preis für den Öijared Golfklub und wurden durch die Medien sehr bekannt.

FJ Das Büro wuchs dann recht rasch zu einem Großbüro?

GW Über den Auftrag für den Golfklub kam die Verbindung zu der Pharmafirma Astra-Zeneca, damals noch Hässle, bei der wir 1989 den Wettbewerb für das Firmengelände in Mölndal gewannen. Wir waren voll ausgelastet, ein junges Büro und eines der ersten in Schweden, das voll computerisiert arbeitete. Als 1990 die Rezession einsetzte, waren wir in einer guten Position mit dem größten Bauprojekt Westschwedens und konnten daran in den neunziger Jahren kontinuierlich arbeiten.

AstraZeneca, wiederum mit dem Kasper Salin Preis bedacht, zog dann Ericsson nach sich, heute mein wichtigster Klient. Endgültig etabliert haben wir uns mit dem Gewinn der Wettbewerbe für die schwedische Botschaft in Berlin und für das Olympiastadion in Stockholm (es war nett, gegen Kontrahenten wie Rem Koolhaas und Santiago Calatrava zu gewinnen). Seitdem haben wir auch die Kontakte zu Politikern und Offiziellen in Stockholm.

FJ Bei all Ihren Projekten wird kein Individualstil erkennbar, keine durchgängige Architektursprache. Wollen Sie keine Marke Wingårdh entwickeln?

GW Nein, nur etwas Kalkstein, der immer wieder auftaucht ... Jeder andere entwickelt eine eigene Architektur. Aber wir haben uns immer für die Bewegung, das Fließende interessiert, lassen das Äußere vom Inneren kontrollieren, sind immer darauf aus, jede Aufgabe neu zu lösen. Bei AstraZeneca dachten alle, wir würden den Konferenz- und Restaurantbereich wieder wie beim Golfklub um den Hügel legen, aber wir experimentierten mit Gabionen, um dem Konferenzbereich etwas Schweres, Steinernes gegenüber der leichten Aluminium-Architektur der Labors zu geben. Jedes Projekt ist für uns eine Gelegenheit zu forschen und neue Wege zu finden. Und so kommt es, dass es unser Stil ist, keinen Stil zu haben.

FJ Eine Konstante in Ihrer Arbeit ist jedoch die ökologische Orientierung. Ist das in Schweden üblich, oder ist das Ihr individuelles Engagement?

GW Ja, das machen alle, aber noch nicht so lange. Es hat viel damit zu tun, dass ich die Universität verließ, als wir die Ölkrise hatten, denn damals lag der Fokus auf ökologischem Denken. Als ich die Gelegenheit bekam, den Golfklub zu entwerfen, verließ ich den Postmodernismus der Interieurarchitektur und ließ mich von Emilio Ambasz inspirieren, der seine Gebäude in der Erde vergrub und mit Grün überdeckte. Dadurch wurde der Baukonzern Skanska auf mich aufmerksam, förderte meine ökologische Ausrichtung und wollte mit mir nachhaltige Projekte realisieren. Letztlich wurde nichts daraus, doch der Manager ist heute Geschäftsführer bei Folkhem, mit denen wir viele Wohnbauprojekte realisieren.

Als ich 1993 mein eigenes Haus baute, gab es noch keine ökologischen Vorgänger. Es war deshalb sehr interessant, ein Haus ohne Plastikmembranen, mit kontrollierter Lüftung und begrüntem Dach zu bauen. Das war sehr erfolgreich.

Als wir das Ale Gymnasium bauten, gab es gerade Diskussionen um die gesundheitlichen Probleme für Schüler und Lehrer in den billig gebauten Schulen und wir bemühten uns um gesunde Materialien und gute Lüftung. Seit wir die lüftungstechnisch hochinstallierten AstraZeneca-Gebäude geplant haben, haben wir beste Verbindungen zu den entsprechenden Fachleuten und Firmen.

was that I shared a seventh prize with Sigurd Lewerentz! I took on my first employee in 1982. A year later, we received the commission to redesign an old-fashioned hotel in Malmö. I realised the work with an emphasis on quality craftsmanship, which wasn't customary in Sweden at the time. That led to a subsequent commission for the Hilton Slussen in Stockholm. A period of travelling between Göteborg and Stockholm began, because along with that contract I opened a Stockholm branch of the office in 1985. We were awarded the Kasper Salin Prize for Öijared Golf Club in 1988 and became very well-known due to the media.

FJ Then the office grew big very quickly?

GW That contract for the golf club meant that we developed connections with the pharmaceutical company AstraZeneca, still Hässle at that time, and we won the competition to design its company site in Mölndal in 1989. We had more than enough to do—a young office and one of the first in Sweden to be fully computerised. When the recession began in 1990, we were in a good position, having the biggest construction project in western Sweden at the time; we were able to work on it continually throughout the nineties.

AstraZeneca, which received the Kasper Salin Prize as well, led on to Ericsson, which is my most important client today. Finally, we established ourselves firmly by winning the competitions for the Swedish embassy in Berlin and the Olympic Stadium in Stockholm (it was nice to win against competitors like Rem Koolhaas and Santiago Calatrava). Since then we have had contacts with politicians and officials in Stockholm, of course.

FJ In all your projects, no individual style becomes perceptible; there is no consistent architectural language. Don't you want to develop a Wingårdh brand?

GW No, just a bit of limestone that keeps on turning up … Every other architect develops his or her own architecture. But we have always been interested in motion, in the flow; we allow the exterior to be guided from within, and our aim is always to solve each task in a new way. At AstraZeneca we all thought that we would probably arrange the conference and restaurant area around the hill, as we had done at the golf club; but instead we experimented with gabions to give the conference area something weighty—the solidity of stone in contrast to the light aluminium architecture of the laboratory. We regard every project as an opportunity to research and find new approaches. That is how it has come about that our style is to have no recognisable style.

FJ But one constant in your work is its ecological orientation. Is that the done thing in Sweden, or is it your individual commitment?

GW Yes, everyone does it, but they haven't been doing it for so long. It has a lot to do with the fact that I left university during the oil crisis, because at that time the focus was on ecological thinking. When I got the opportunity to design the golf club, I abandoned the post-modernism of interior design and allowed myself to be inspired by Emilio Ambasz, who buried his buildings in the ground and covered them over with greenery. It was this that earned me the attention of Skanska Construction Company, which promoted my ecological orientation and at the time intended to collaborate with me on sustainable projects. Nothing came of that in the end, but today the manager is CEO at Folkhem, a customer with whom we realise many housing construction projects.

When I built my own house in 1993, there were no ecological predecessors. That made it very interesting to construct a house without plastic membranes, with controlled ventilation and a grass roof. It was a great success.

When we built the grammar school in Ale, current discussions were focused on the health problems for pupils and teachers in cheaply constructed schools and we made an effort to use healthy materials and provide good ventilation. Since planning the AstraZeneca building with its superior quality ventilation technology, we have had ideal links to the corresponding specialists and companies.

FJ Gibt es spezifisch schwedische Elemente in der Architektur und gibt es die auch bei Ihnen?

GW Die meisten schwedischen Architekten sind an den sozialen Kontakten der Menschen interessiert, das ist in ihnen tief verwurzelt. Bei AstraZeneca zum Beispiel gibt es dieses Rückgrat als Erschließungszone, nicht pompös, eher intim und auf diese Weise eine sehr schwedische Lösung. Hier treffen sich die Mitarbeiter zwangsläufig, es gibt Reibung wie in einer engen venezianischen Gasse und dadurch Kommunikation. All diese Dinge, die Pausenecken oder die Frage, wo triffst du deinen Boss, beim Mittagessen, in der Kantine usw., werden von den ausländischen Auftraggebern nachgefragt; sie sind schwedisch.

FJ Welche Rolle spielt die Moderne in Schweden? Gab es in Schweden auch den postmodernen Bruch?

GW Bis Mitte der sechziger Jahre gab es eine sehr schöne moderne Tradition. Dann gab es eine große Landflucht und in den Städten wurde viel abgebrochen und von den Baukonzernen mit ihren verbündeten Architekten durch rationalistische, gesichtslose Bauten ersetzt. Niemand liebte diese Architektur und die Architekten verloren in der Bevölkerung das Vertrauen. Sie hatten in den siebziger Jahren eine schwache Position und niemand glaubte ihnen mehr. Stattdessen begrüßte man traditionelle Architektur, zum Beispiel das Ethnografische Museum in Form einer rot gestrichenen Holzhütte. Nur ganz wenige Architekten konnten die moderne Position verteidigen. Lewerentz baute in jener Zeit seine wichtigsten Werke. In den frühen achtziger Jahren war das Land reif für die Postmoderne. Meine zweite Villa wird immer als Beginn der Postmoderne in Schweden bezeichnet. Die Rezession Anfang der neunziger Jahre bahnte dann dem Modernismus wieder den Weg.

FJ In jüngerer Zeit ist viel von *icons* die Rede, von *signature architecture*. Gibt es auch in Schweden eine Nachfrage nach solchen *icons*?

GW Nein. Es gab Möglichkeiten, etwa als das Modern Museum in Stockholm geplant wurde, was dann Moneo mit einem sehr ruhigen Entwurf gebaut hat, oder die Erweiterung der Asplund-Bibliothek, wobei es darum ging, den Altbau nicht zu unterwerfen. Auch diesen Wettbewerb gewann ein sehr ruhiger Entwurf aus Deutschland. Erst jetzt, in den letzten Jahren, gab es auch ein Verlangen nach flamboyanten Gebäuden, aber nur der Turm von Calatrava in Malmö ist realisiert worden.

FJ Gibt es Architekten, die Sie besonders bewundern und von denen Sie sich sehr beeinflussen ließen?

GW Mein Problem ist, dass ich ständig von jedermann beeinflusst werde. Als Student bewunderte ich die alten Meister Le Corbusier, Frank Lloyd Wright, Oscar Niemeyer und gab Entwürfe ab in der Art, wie Niemeyer, wie Rossi sie vorgelegt hätten. Es waren immer die Architekten, die viel verändert haben; heute sind es Schweizer Architekten, die andere, sehr verschiedene Wege gehen. Bei Herzog & de Meuron ist das zu sehen, auch bei Peter Zumthor, dass die Projekte sehr unterschiedlich sind.

Ich bin viel in Deutschland gereist, habe die Bauten von Scharoun gesehen und liebe den fließenden Raum, der auch bei Behnisch anzutreffen ist. Scharouns Bauten, nicht zuletzt die Staatsbibliothek, gehören zu den interessantesten Bauten weltweit. Klassische, symmetrische Architektur mag ich nicht so sehr.

FJ Wie ist es mit den Materialien? Kommt der Kalkstein, den Sie oft einsetzen, immer aus derselben Gegend?

GW Mir gefällt, wie das Material altert. Man kann aus Kalkstein alle Formen machen. Es kommt vielleicht auch daher, dass ich an einem Berg mit einem Bach aufwuchs und dort immer mit Kalkstein spielte. Ich habe also eine gewisse Affinität zu dem Material und habe mir einmal vorgestellt, nur mit diesem einen Stoff zu arbeiten. Materialien spielen bei uns allgemein eine große Rolle.

FJ Sie arbeiten auch gerne mit Holz, ist das eine schwedische Tradition?

FJ Are there any specifically Swedish elements in architecture, and can they be found in your work?

GW Most Swedish architects are interested in people's social contacts; that is deeply rooted in their work. At AstraZeneca, for example, the circulation area is a kind of backbone—nothing pompous, but rather intimate and a very Swedish solution in that sense. The employees will inevitably encounter one another here: there will be contact like there is in a narrow Venetian alleyway, and there is communication as a result. Foreign clients are puzzled by all these things—like corners for breaks, or they ask where you meet your boss, at lunch, in the canteen etc. Such matters are Swedish.

FJ What role does Modernism play in Sweden? Was there a post-modern break in Sweden as well?

GW A very attractive modernist tradition existed until the mid-sixties. Then there was a great exodus from the countryside and a lot of building in the cities was demolished and replaced by rationalist, faceless structures made by construction companies and their allied architects. No one loved that architecture and the architects lost people's trust. They had a weak position in the seventies, no one believed them anymore. Instead, people welcomed traditional architecture like the Ethnographic Museum, which took the form of a red-painted wooden cabin. Only very few architects were able to defend the modernist position. Lewerentz built his most important works at that time. In the early eighties the country was ready for Post-Modernism. My second villa is always regarded as the onset of Post-Modernism in Sweden. Then the recession at the beginning of the nineties paved the way for a return of Modernism.

FJ Recently there has been much talk of icons, of signature architecture. Is there a demand for such icons in Sweden?

GW No. There have been opportunities, e.g., when the Modern Museum in Stockholm was planned, but then Moneo realised it with a very serene design; or the extension of the Asplund Library, where it was important not to subjugate the old building. This competition was also won by a very tranquil design from Germany. Only now, in recent years, has there been a demand for flamboyant buildings as well, but only the tower by Calatrava has actually been realised in Malmö.

FJ Are there architects that you admire especially, allowing them to influence you a lot?

GW My problem is that I am constantly being influenced by everyone. As a student I admired the old masters Le Corbusier, Frank Lloyd Wright or Oscar Niemeyer and submitted designs reminiscent of those that Niemeyer or Rossi had presented. It was always architects who had changed a lot; today it is Swiss architects who take different, very diverse paths. It is easy to see that the projects of Herzog & de Meuron and also Peter Zumthor are very different, for example.

I travelled a lot in Germany; I saw buildings by Scharoun, and I love the fluid space that one can also encounter in Behnisch's work. Scharoun's buildings, not least the state library, are among the most interesting buildings in the world. I don't like classical, symmetrical architecture as much.

FJ What about the materials? Does the limestone that you often employ always come from the same area?

GW I like the way in which the material ages. It is possible to create all sorts of forms from limestone. Perhaps it is because I grew up by a mountain with a stream and I always played with the limestone there. So I have a certain affinity with the material; I once imagined working with this material alone. Generally speaking, the materials play a very important role for us.

FJ You also like to work with wood; is that a Swedish tradition?

GW That happens on various levels. In the case of private houses, wooden construction is a question of economy and also connected to tradition. In addition, it leads to a warm

GW Das geschieht auf verschiedenen Ebenen. Beim Privathaus ist Holzbau eine ökonomische Frage und mit der Tradition verbunden. Außerdem erhält man eine warme Atmosphäre. Wir verwenden Holz in vielfältiger Weise und lassen uns immer etwas Neues einfallen. An Holz gefällt uns, dass es immer lebendig wirkt, weil es nicht perfekt ist, das gilt auch für den Naturstein. Bei der Schule in Nödige sahen wir das Holz als Untergrund für die Schüler, die ihre Namen einritzen, quasi als eine Art Tattoo oder eine Gebrauchsschicht. Nur einmal, bei der Betonvilla, haben wir wirklich Perfektion angestrebt – eine Ausnahme.

FJ Die Materialpalette ist also Beton, Holz, Kalkstein und Glas. Stahl spielt keine Rolle? Ist das ideologisch bedingt?

GW Unsere Ideologie ist, zu lernen, immer etwas Neues herauszufinden und nicht notwendigerweise viel zu wiederholen.

FJ Wie kann man Ihre Architektur lehren? Was geben Sie an die Studenten weiter?

GW Ich lehre durch das Stellen kritischer Fragen. Bei jedem Vorschlag schwache und starke Stellen auffinden, das kann einen überallhin bringen. Es ist wie bei uns im Studio, die Ergebnisse sind unvorhersehbar.

FJ Haben Sie sich schriftlich theoretisch über Architektur geäußert, an der Hochschule zum Beispiel?

GW Niemals. Ich versuche, in meinen Vorlesungen sehr persönlich zu sein, meine Ideen zu präsentieren. Es gibt lediglich eine Broschüre *Reflections over the Architecture* zur Ausstellung „Eleven Houses", die einige private Gedanken und Empfindungen zur Architektur auf eine eher poetische, philosophische Art präsentiert.

FJ Sie sind sehr ortstreu, sind vom Studium bis heute in Göteborg geblieben und haben das meiste hier gebaut. Gibt es Ambitionen, nun doch mehr im Ausland zu bauen?

GW Der beste Bauplatz liegt zwischen meinem Studio und meiner Wohnung. Idealerweise sollten wir natürlich nur in Göteborg bauen. Wir haben ein Büro in Stockholm, weil es dort eine Vielzahl interessanter Möglichkeiten gibt. An Wettbewerben im Ausland haben wir nur in Deutschland teilgenommen. Der Grund war, dass wir durch die Botschaft in Berlin überzeugt waren vom hohen Qualitätsstandard des deutschen Handwerks und vom Respekt, der uns entgegengebracht wurde. Wir haben deshalb weitergemacht, weil alles in Deutschland der schwedischen Kultur so nahe ist. Dennoch sind die Unterschiede, die Nuancen darin interessant, wie deutsche Leute denken oder Leute in Dänemark oder Finnland, wo wir auch hin und wieder für schwedische Klienten gebaut haben.

An Wettbewerben in anderen, vor allem skandinavischen Ländern haben wir teilgenommen, wenn es sich um schwedische Bauherren gehandelt hat. Die Einladung, ein Museum im Zentrum von Paris zu bauen, würden wir natürlich nicht ausschließen.

Als Ericsson eine neue Hauptverwaltung in Peking plante, luden sie uns neben englischen, australischen und amerikanischen Architekten zum Wettbewerb ein und wir nahmen teil (und gewannen), nicht weil wir den Wunsch hatten, in China zu bauen, sondern weil wir uns mit Ericsson verbunden fühlen. Es ist ja doch ermüdend, in Nah- oder Fernost zu bauen, ständig durch die Welt zu fliegen, das bringt keine Lebensqualität. Deshalb bauen wir gerne in Göteborg.

atmosphere. We use wood in a wide range of ways and are always thinking of new ideas. The thing we like about wood is that it always appears to be alive, because it is not perfect; and that is also true of natural stone. At the school in Nödige we saw the wood as a background for the pupils who carved their names into it, almost as a kind of tattoo or a layer of use. Only once, in the case of the concrete villa, did we really aim for perfection—that was an exception.

FJ So the range of materials is concrete, wood, limestone, and glass. Steel doesn't play a part at all? Is that determined by ideology?

GW It is our ideology to learn, to be always finding out something new and not necessarily to repeat much.

FJ How is it possible to teach your architecture? What do you pass on to the students?

GW I teach by asking critical questions. If you point out the strong and weak points of every suggestion, that can take you anywhere. It is like our work in the studio; the results are unpredictable.

FJ Have you written anything theoretical about architecture—at the university, for example?

GW Never. I try to be very personal in my lectures, to present my own ideas. All that exists is a brochure *Reflexions over the Architecture* about the exhibition "Eleven Houses", which presents some private thoughts and feelings concerning architecture in a rather poetic, philosophical way.

FJ You are very loyal to place. From your studies to the present day you have remained in Göteborg and have even realised most of your projects here. Do you have any ambitions to build abroad more often?

GW The ideal construction site for me would be between my studio and my apartment. Ideally, of course, we should only build in Göteborg. We have an office in Stockholm, because there are a large number of interesting possibilities there. The only competitions abroad that we have entered were in Germany—the reason being that the Berlin embassy project convinced us of the very high standards of German craftsmanship, and we encountered respect from people there. That is why we continued—because everything in Germany is so close to Swedish culture. Nevertheless, it is interesting to see the differences, the nuances in the way German people think, or folk in Denmark or Finland, where we have also built for Swedish clients occasionally.

We have participated in competitions in other, primarily Scandinavian countries when the building clients were Swedish. Of course, we wouldn't refuse an invitation to build a museum in the centre of Paris!

When Ericsson was planning new headquarters in Peking, they invited us to take part in a competition alongside British, Australian and American architects, and we did so (and won)—not because we had any desire to build in China but because we felt a bond with Ericsson. But it's tiring to build in the Middle or Far East, to be constantly flying across the world; it doesn't improve your quality of life. That's why we like to build in Göteborg.